Financing social security: The options

Financing social security: The options

An international analysis

International Labour Office   Geneva

ISBN 92-2-103232-9 (limp cover)
ISBN 92-2-103634-0 (hard cover)

First published 1984

Originally published in French under the title:
Sécurité sociale: quelle méthode de financement? (ISBN 92-2-203232-2)

Printed in Switzerland

FOREWORD

One of the most urgent questions facing social security today is that of its financing methods. The problem has been made all the more acute by the current economic crisis: whereas the national product is marking time, expenditure is constantly rising. In the course of its 100 years of existence, social security has developed considerably and changed profoundly. Today, it has to be asked whether traditional financing methods will suffice much longer to meet its rising costs and at the same time satisfy economic demands and the need to ensure that social charges are psychologically and politically acceptable, equitably distributed and easy to collect, or whether the time has not come to turn to other methods.

The debate on this subject in the industrial countries is of the greatest interest to the International Labour Organisation. This is so, in the first place, because the main sources of financial support for social security–governments, employers and workers–are represented on an equal footing in the ILO which, by reason of its tripartite structure, is undoubtedly a most suitable forum for the discussion of these matters. Secondly, the volume of the transfers made by the social security systems successively set up in industrial countries has become so large that methods of financing are no longer "neutral" in respect of other social phenomena of major concern to the ILO, beginning with employment. The relation between direct wages and social wages appears in another light as soon as the latter take on such profound significance for the workers' welfare.

Since its foundation in 1919, the ILO has been constantly concerned with the financing of social benefits, at first in the form of compulsory social insurance, then, after the Second World War, in the broader framework of modern social security policy. The large number of international studies it has carried out on actuarial techniques, financing methods, the investment of funds and macro-economic aspects of financing bear witness to this concern. Since 1950 the International Labour Office has carried out a periodical inquiry into the cost of social security, providing complete series of statistics on the receipts and expenditure of the different schemes

v

in operation in its member States,[1] information which is indispensable for the quantitative, sectoral and global analysis of financing systems, whether from the point of view of their structure by source of funds, or from that of their macro-economic effects.

The ILO's decision at the beginning of the 1980s to resume its study of financing methods is prompted in the first place by the fact that the terms of the problem have changed in the past few years. The economic downturn in many countries and the rise in unemployment have led the authorities to speculate on the possible effect on employment of social security contributions based on wages. Even if the economic crisis had not given rise to such heart-searching, the time had come to re-examine the structure of financing, as the extension of coverage to the whole population had shown that the financial model inherited from social insurance was no longer suitable, especially for the protection of self-employed persons and the non-working population.

It was for this reason that the ILO decided to convene a tripartite meeting of experts at the end of 1981 to review past developments and identify trends in the light of national and international experience.[2]

This publication includes the most important of the papers prepared for the meeting. The choice has fallen, on the one hand, on those of international scope and, on the other, on a series of national reports describing the position adopted in the countries concerned regarding the criteria on which a rationalisation of social security financing—much desired but seldom achieved—should be based.

From a perusal of this volume the reader will observe that the pursuit of efficiency in social security financing cannot be divorced from the appraisal of its methods, particularly in respect of their transparency, equity and compatibility with requirements for economic stability. The more closely such financing methods are adapted to economic conditions, the better they are understood and the more widely they are accepted, the more productive they will doubtless be. In this respect, the way in which they are applied is no less important than their amount.

Notes

[1] The results of the most recent inquiry have been published in ILO: *The cost of social security: Tenth international inquiry, 1975-77* (Geneva, 1981).

[2] Meeting of Experts on Social Security Financing, Geneva, 30 November-3 December 1981.

CONTENTS

Tables

Figures

PART ONE

DEVELOPMENT AND PRESENT TRENDS

METHODS OF FINANCING SOCIAL SECURITY IN INDUSTRIAL COUNTRIES: AN INTERNATIONAL ANALYSIS

Pierre Mouton *

THE ORIGIN OF FINANCING METHODS

The institution of social security at the end of the Second World War did not bring about any radical revolution in financing methods. The social security systems set up in the post-war period simply took over and combined, in varying degrees and ways, the methods which had been used by the two earlier major forms of social protection–social insurance and non-contributory benefits–which have now been regrouped under social security.

The social insurance model

The German system of social insurance which was set up by Bismarck originated in the voluntary funds to which workers could contribute as a way of protecting themselves in old age and in the event of sickness, invalidity or unemployment. At the beginning, the general opinion seems to have been that the social insurance system had simply generalised and made obligatory an institution which had previously been voluntary, so that the workers' participation in financing was taken for granted. The introduction of a compulsory contribution borne by employers was a major step forward in social progress, although Prussia, in 1849 and above all in 1854, had already established regulations for contingency funds and made it obligatory for employers to participate in financing by contributions of up to as much as half of those provided by the workers. Such a contribution was moreover necessary, since the workers covered by the obligatory scheme (which applied only to the poorest workers) were unable to finance the scheme alone. Nevertheless, as regards sickness insurance, the employer's contribution represented only half that of the worker (equality of contributions was subsequently established as regards old-age and invalidity insurance); even in the case of accident insurance, for which the prin-

---

* International Labour Office.

ciple of employer responsibility had already been accepted, the idea of a worker contribution was initially put forward (it was ultimately rejected except in Austria, where it was introduced and maintained until 1917).[1]

Provision for state participation had been made only in the case of old-age and invalidity insurance, in the form of a fixed annual subsidy granted for each pension provided, "in order to satisfy the just claim of the worker to the reasonable degree of relief".[2]

The widespread influence of the Bismarckian model, including its financing methods, is well known. The countries which drew upon the model had recourse to the same sources of financing, although in forms and proportions which varied according to numerous specific and complex factors, including the evolution of the respective strengths of workers' organisations, employers' associations and political parties.

Unemployment insurance developed outside Germany went through a number of stages of its own—initially the cost was borne entirely by the workers, then there was participation by the public authorities—before the financing was put on a tripartite basis, as in old-age and disability insurance, under the British Act of 1911, which served to a large extent as the model for the other national systems subsequently established. In Great Britain, too, the law on public sickness insurance adopted in the same year applied the principle of tripartite financing.

In this way, a practice marked by the circumstances which conditioned the original social insurance schemes, the foundations of which were largely experimental, gradually became generalised and organised on a systematic basis.[3] There was no genuine financial doctrine available upon which to base a model for social insurance schemes and it was only later that attempts were made to evolve such a doctrine, in particular by endeavouring to justify the methods used, as was done for example in the memoranda of various social insurance Acts. The justifications thus put forward as regards the sources of financing of social insurance—or some of them at least—are still being advanced today; it would therefore be useful to review these arguments briefly here.[4]

Turning first of all to contributions from insured persons, it was argued that such contributions were justified in as far as the workers' responsibility might be involved, at least in part, in the occurrence of certain contingencies. At the same time, since social insurance requires that the benefits granted should clearly be a right (rather than a form of social assistance), the contributions from insured persons were the counterpart of this right and their payment thus protected the dignity of the beneficiary. Furthermore, compulsory contributions from the insured persons were considered to be a way of encouraging them to save by making them aware of the uncertainty of their future (from the point of view of the persons protected, social insurance has to some extent already taken the place of individual savings). It was also argued that the payment of contributions gave insured persons a right to participate in the management of the social in-

4

surance scheme. Finally, it was considered that the financial participation of insured persons would help to ensure more economical management of the scheme by encouraging participants to avoid excessive expenditure.

Likewise, several arguments were put forward to justify financial contributions from the employers. First of all, such participation is based on the principle of the responsibility of the employer for both the maintenance of his "human capital" when this is affected by the occurrence of certain contingencies and the actual occurrence of such contingencies (occupational hazards first, but also, to some extent, unemployment, sickness and premature invalidity). It is also justified by the advantages which employers can expect to obtain from social insurance (improved quality of work and stability of labour, contribution to good labour relations). As in the case of insured persons, the payment of contributions by employers gave them rights in the management of the scheme.

As regards contributions from the public authorities, they constituted, first of all, a moral obligation, since the public authorities are responsible for the protection of the economically weak members of the community. Besides, it was argued that the State was also partly responsible for the occurrence of certain contingencies such as unemployment or sickness. A further justification was that the operation of social insurance schemes reduced the cost of public assistance. Finally, the financial intervention of the State seemed to be a practical necessity where funds were insufficient or when low contributive capacity of certain categories of workers had to be remedied.

All these and many other arguments were opposed. To give only one example, workers in a large number of countries opposed the system of contributory insurance, arguing that their wages were inadequate, and contesting the concept of justifying the right to benefits by the payment of contributions.

In the period between the two world wars, the ILO, in its efforts to establish an international legislative model based upon the European social insurance schemes and to disseminate this model among its member States, devoted much attention to the question of financing. Since tripartite financing was found to be the method most frequently used in national legislation, the ILO gave its support to this system (except for accident insurance, where costs were to be borne exclusively by the employer, in virtue of the principle of occupational risk). The arguments put forward in 1925 to justify the use of the three financing sources were as follows: employers are clearly interested in being able to count on a regular and ample supply of vigorous manpower; the workers are necessarily concerned to make some provision against the insecurity of their future; and, as for the public authorities, it is incumbent on them to improve public health and hygiene, which are important factors in national prosperity.[5] The idea of a tripartite financing structure was embodied in the early international labour Conventions concerning old-age pensions, invalidity benefits and death grants and (less precisely) sickness insurance. However, the ILO studies carried out during those years [6] also noted that the distribution of the cost of social insurance was, from the economic standpoint, a question of organisation rather than of principle and that no logical criterion had so far been established for determining this distribution (except in cases of employment injuries, where the very clear legal principle of the employers' liability had been accepted). These studies showed that it was difficult in the other branches to establish rational criteria for determining the proportions in which the contributions should be distributed: "One reasonable criterion would be to distribute the cost according to the share of responsibility of each of the parties for the risks; but probably the shares would be estimated very differently by each of the parties concerned."[7] Another possible criterion, that of the advantages the employer could expect to derive from participation, did not produce any better results. Moreover, it was pointed out that the rational distribution of cost was made all the more difficult by the operation of the economic phenomenon of "incidence".

Thus, although the search for a satisfactory doctrine upon which to base the financing of social insurance did not meet with any real success, the practices which emerged from the traditions and experiences of the early social insurance schemes became axiomatic, despite the sometimes inconclusive character of subsequent attempts to rationalise them.

These principles have not, however, been universally accepted. Thus, the USSR has chosen to follow a different path, adopting a unified system of financing for all branches, based exclusively on employers' contributions (immediately after the October Revolution, workers' contributions, for which provision had been made in the previous legislation of 1912 and 1917, were suppressed).

The development of non-contributory benefit schemes, which will be examined below, was also contrary to these principles.

Non-contributory benefit schemes

With this type of benefit, the cost is borne entirely by the public authorities (the State or local communities). The system was based upon the idea that the community as a whole (at the national or local level) was responsible for coming to the assistance of those of its members in need, the individual being able to claim, as a right, that the State should intervene on his or her behalf–an idea which had already been included in the French Constitution of 24 June 1793.

The system of non-contributory benefits derived from poor relief, although it was clearly distinguished from the latter by the introduction of the concept of the right to benefits. It was first applied in Denmark, a country with a predominantly agricultural population (in contrast to that of the Germany of Bismarck which was in the midst of industrialisation) where an Act of 1891 established the right to pensions for all persons subject to various qualifying conditions, in particular as regards means.

The logic governing the financing of non-contributory schemes–which originally concerned above all pensions–was set forth in the following terms in an ILO study: "Non-contributory pensions, whether for the aged, invalid or blind or for mothers with dependent children, are payable when the risk covered materialises, provided that the qualifying conditions are fulfilled. Since all classes of the population are exposed to these risks, every member of society may be regarded as a potential beneficiary–as a person who may fulfil the qualifying conditions. Consequently, the resources needed to finance non-contributory pensions must be supplied by society as a whole." [8] In most cases, these resources were obtained exclusively from ordinary taxes and quite often the cost of benefits was borne jointly by the central government and the local authorities. However, in some States, particularly in the Americas, the cost of pensions was met by the proceeds of special direct or indirect taxes.

The system of non-contributory pensions, which by the end of the nineteenth and beginning of the twentieth century had been developed in several countries (Australia, Belgium, France, New Zealand . . .), was subsequently extended to other branches such as maternity allowances in Germany and, above all, unemployment benefit in many countries from the 1930s on and, in 1937, medical care benefit in the USSR. On the whole, however, before the Second World War the non-contributory system remained of secondary importance in relation to social insurance.

Non-contributory pensions were often regarded as a transitory measure, destined sooner or later to make way for pensions insurance.[9] In fact, several national legislations co-ordinated non-contributory pensions with the social insurance systems which were subsequently established, as in Denmark where these pensions were reserved for persons who contributed under the national sickness and invalidity insurance schemes (the scope of which was indeed very large). Other countries integrated the two systems; in the United Kingdom, non-contributory pensions were guaranteed automatically to persons insured under the new pension insurance scheme set up for wage earners, whereas non-insured persons continued to be paid pensions in accordance with the earlier regulations.

A particularly interesting development as regards financing was that which occurred in the period immediately preceding the Second World War in the non-contributory pension schemes in Norway and the non-contributory benefits in New Zealand. In Norway, in 1936, the pensions formerly paid by the communes were made a national service, financed not only by public funds (from the State and the communes) but also by a special contribution levied on all individuals and corporate bodies in proportion to their income, and collected by the tax services (in Sweden national old-age and invalidity insurance schemes had already been similarly financed since 1913). In New Zealand, in 1938, the existing non-contributory benefits were grouped with a series of new benefits in a national scheme financed in part directly by the State and in part by a contribution levied on all adults on the basis of their income.

In neither case did the conversion to a contributory system radically affect the other aspects of the previous system (in particular the conditions of entitlement to benefits and the calculation of the latter on the basis of needs rather than contribution periods). Although the new method of financing resembled that of social insurance schemes by its contributory nature, it was markedly different in as far as, first, the contribution levied on all adults was calculated on the basis of their total income from all sources and not only on their income from work (however, for a large number of wage earners who have no other income than that derived from their work, this special tax can be likened to the traditional workers' contribution). Secondly, the employers participated on an equal footing with other taxpayers, with contributions calculated on the basis of their own income, independently of the total amount of wages paid to their staff. In fact, financing continued to be provided by the community as a whole, as in the case of non-contributory benefits, but in two distinct ways: resources came from both the general revenue of the State (and, where applicable, from the local authorities) as well as from a specially earmarked contribution which was superimposed on the general tax system but paid by the same taxpayers.

Thus this new financing method obscured the dividing line between the two streams of social protection which were to converge and form the social security systems. In the following section consideration will be given to the effects on financing of the advent of social security at the beginning of the 1940s.

Financing methods and the advent of social security

The new concept which gave rise to social security systems, as set out in the Beveridge Report of 1942,[10] the Income Security Recommendation (No. 67) and the Medical Care Recommendation (No. 69), adopted by the International Labour Conference in 1944, approached the question of financing in different ways.

The Beveridge Report recommended a twofold method: financing for family benefits and the national health service by the Treasury, that is to say, recourse to national solidarity; financing for replacement benefits mainly by contributions from the insured persons and, in the case of wage earners, from their employers, in accordance with the classic principle of social insurance.

Recommendation No. 67, which stresses the prime importance of social insurance, sets forth in Paragraph 26 a series of guiding principles relating to the classic tripartite structure of financing: "The cost of benefits, including the cost of administration, should be distributed among insured persons, employers and taxpayers, in such a way as to be equitable to insured persons and to avoid hardship to insured persons of small means or any disturbance to production." The suggestions made concerning the application of these principles specify in particular that employers should be required to bear the entire cost of compensation for employment injuries, that they should contribute not less than half the total cost of the other benefits and that the community should bear the cost of benefits which cannot be met by contributions, i.e. for example, the contribution deficits resulting from bringing persons into insurance when already elderly, the contingent liability involved in guaranteeing the payment of basic invalidity, old-age and survivors' benefits and the payment of adequate maternity benefit, the liability resulting from the extended payment of unemployment benefit when unemployment persists at a high level and subsidies to the insurance of self-employed persons of small means.

In Recommendation No. 69, which stipulates that medical care may be provided by a social insurance medical care service or a public medical care service, a distinction is made between the two services in terms of the way in which they are financed. As regards the social insurance medical care service, it is logical that the financing should be by means of contributions, although the instrument stipulates that the contribution paid by an insured person should be such as can be borne without hardship, that employers should be required to pay part of the contribution on behalf of persons employed by them, that persons whose income does not exceed subsistence level should not be required to pay an insurance contribution and that the cost of the medical care service not covered by contributions should be borne by the taxpayers. The cost of the medical care service, as a public service, should be met out of public funds; where the whole population is covered, the service may be financed out of general revenue or it may be appropriate to finance the service by a special progressively graded tax from which persons whose income does not exceed subsistence level should be exempt.

With the advent of social security a new concept of social protection came to the fore; a new doctrine, in many other respects coherent and well developed, took shape but without bringing about any radical revolution in financing methods. Under the social security system, the earlier fund-raising methods were retained and recombined. While there was an evident desire, particularly in the Beveridge Report, to have greater recourse to national solidarity, especially as regards benefits granted to the population as a whole, the influence of the traditional social insurance financing methods remained predominant.

Although it never proved possible to establish a real social insurance financial doctrine, a body of principles based on practice, and moreover fairly widely accepted, did at least provide a relatively strict framework and served as a model for the national legislations of a number of countries. As regards the financing of social security, no such strict rules concerning the origin of resources, which could act as a model, appear to have been established. In the words of a study published at the time, "from the moment at which the problem of social security is regarded as one to be solved by general policy and under a general scheme, it is comparatively unimportant whether the money destined to keep the scheme in operation ... has been obtained by means of contributions or drawn direct from public funds ... it is only a question of convenience, apart from considerations of economic policy or industrial morale, whether the resources necessary to meet social security expenditure in the aggregate should be collected by one method rather than another ...".[11] This freedom as regards the choice of financing methods is clearly reflected in the Social Security (Minimum Standards) Convention, 1952 (No. 102), which, in Article 71, simply states that the cost of benefits must be borne collectively by insurance contributions or taxation, or both, in a manner that avoids placing too heavy a burden on persons of small means. The only specific provision concerns the division of contributions between the employer and the worker; the total contribution borne by the latter must not exceed 50 per cent of the total of the resources allocated to the protection of employees and the members of their families.

Examination of the financing methods used in the early social security systems reveals both their fidelity to the past and the frequent absence of any theoretical preoccupations. In order to cover the new expenditure resulting from the establishment of these systems in the difficult post-war economic situation, recourse was frequently had to pre-existing schemes as well as a wide range of other methods.[12] Although there was no sudden change, a gradual evolution did take place, in which several innovative trends should be distinguished.

There was first of all some (albeit limited) degree of development in the unified system of financing for all the branches, already adopted in 1932 in the USSR, as noted earlier, with the consequent possibility (in the United Kingdom, for example) that the cost of compensation for occupational injuries would no longer be borne solely by the employers but would be shared with the workers, contrary to the most frequently adopted earlier principles and those of Recommendation No. 67.

The proportion of public funds in the resources of the social security systems increased, particularly in as far as family benefits in several countries such as Canada, Finland, Hungary, Ireland, Norway, Sweden and the United Kingdom were financed out of the national budget. However, this was not always the case: for example, in France social security for non-agricultural workers was financed solely from employers' and workers' contributions from 1945 on, when state subsidies were suppressed. The contribution from the public authorities may take various forms (lump-sum subsidies or subsidies linked to other contributions, reimbursement of certain expenditure, coverage of shortfall in the event of insufficient resources, earmarking of special taxes or levies). In a significant number of countries where the public contribution has increased, it has taken the form of a special tax levied either directly on income as in Argentina, Australia, Finland, New Zealand, Norway or Sweden, or indirectly (tax on tobacco and spirits in Switzerland, levies on ore exports in Bolivia, various special indirect taxes in Greece).

The extension of protection to categories other than wage earners, including persons who are not economically active, and *a fortiori* to the whole of the population, has necessarily entailed a break with the social insurance financing methods established for wage earners (contributions from both employers and employees) and unsuited to self-employed workers or other persons. It was necessary to have recourse to other financing sources (over and above the personal contributions from insured persons) which inevitably had to be calculated on a basis other than that of wages and in many cases were still inadequate to ensure the financing of the scheme.

In countries which continued to make use of contributions from employed persons, there was a tendency to reduce the share paid by the workers, which was compensated by higher contributions from the employers or the State. Moreover, like the USSR, several Eastern European countries completely suppressed all workers' contributions.

DEVELOPMENT OF FINANCING SINCE 1950

The evolution of social security financing since 1950 was marked by the rapid rise in social levies, modifications—often important but not all tending the same way—in the structure of these contributions and a progressive reorganisation of the financing techniques.

The increase in receipts from social charges

A development common to all industrialised countries is the rise in their social security expenditure, which necessitates higher receipts from social charges, obtained either by a widening of the contribution base or an increase in contribution rates, or by the introduction of new methods of levying contributions. The causes of the rise in charges have often been stated—better coverage of social risks by extending the scope of schemes and improving the benefits provided, demographic phenomena such as the ageing of the population, technological developments which, among other reasons, explain the very steep rise in expenditure on health care, effects of the crisis, etc.—and need not be repeated in this study.

The statistical analysis given below (Chapter 2) reflects these developments. It will suffice here to quote a few figures which clearly illustrate how these social contributions have grown and the levels they have attained. As regards, first, the development of resources earmarked for social security expenditure (social insurance and allied schemes only), it can be seen that, at constant 1975 prices, they increased in the period 1960-77 by 2.75 times in the United Kingdom, 3.73 times in the United States, 4.60 times in France, 5.10 times in Sweden and 12.84 times in Japan.

As regards the level attained by social levies, total social security receipts expressed as a proportion of gross domestic product (GDP) exceeded 15 per cent in most industrial countries by 1977, reached 20 per cent in a good third of them and 30 per cent in the Netherlands and Sweden.[13] Since 1977, GDP stagnation coupled with the continued rise in social security expenditure has only further increased this proportion, which in 1960 was less than 17 per cent in all countries and, ten years later, was still below 10 per cent in very many of them. The question of the maximum acceptable rate of such levies has often been asked and is the subject of keen debate but it seems impossible to give a reply which is valid for all countries and all periods.[14] It may simply be noted that all attempts to fix a ceiling for compulsory taxation, social or otherwise, have to date always ended in failure.

How did such a rapid increase in the burden placed on the GDP come about? To the extent that wages have generally risen more rapidly than the GDP, so also have contributions based on wages. An initial explanation can therefore be given in cases where financing is mainly covered by contributions; this passive increase was, however, far from being sufficient. Action had to be taken to balance expenditure, first, by increasing the yield of contributions by modifying their base and rates, and secondly by recourse to supplementary measures.

Increase in contribution rates

Already in 1949 an ILO study had pointed out that "in some cases the total amount (of contributions) expressed as a percentage of wages is higher than ever before".[15] Since then, in most countries which have continued to rely to an important extent on this source of financing, the raising of contribution rates has necessarily remained the chosen method of increasing revenue. In some countries, there have been frequent changes in contribution rates. For example, in France, 22 such changes, including 16 increases, occurred between 1947 and 1981.

In several cases, there has been a major increase in the global rate. In Spain, this rate more than doubled between 1958 and 1979–from 16.35 per cent to 33.85 per cent, excluding employment–and it has risen by more than 50 per cent over the past 30 years in such countries as Austria (workers' scheme)–from between 21.2 and 24 per cent in 1950 to 38.20 per cent in 1979; Belgium (manual wage earners)–from 21 per cent in 1950 to 34.2 per cent in 1980, excluding occupational injuries; the Federal Republic of Germany–from an average of 20 per cent in 1950 to between 33 and 36.1 per cent in 1979; Greece–from 16 per cent in 1950 to between 26.5 and 27 per cent in 1979; Italy (industrial manual workers)–from 32.73 per cent in

1950 to 51.2 per cent in 1979; Japan–from 11 per cent in 1950 to 18.55 per cent in 1979, excluding occupational injuries. In the United States, the contribution rate for the pensions scheme rose from 3 per cent in 1950 to 3.4 per cent in 1982. In the Netherlands, where chronological comparison is difficult because of the integration of insurance against occupational injuries in the other branches in 1967, the rate for which previously varied with the degree of risk involved, it can, however, be noted that contributions which accounted for 24.45 per cent of wages in 1958 (excluding occupational injuries) had risen to 50.91 per cent by 1979. Although the increase has been more moderate in some countries, such as France (general insurance scheme–from 32 per cent in 1950 to 40 per cent in 1981, excluding occupational injuries and unemployment), or Luxembourg (manual workers)–from 20.5 per cent in 1950 to between 24.75 and 26.55 per cent in 1979, excluding occupational injuries–it has, on the contrary, been very rapid recently in other countries; thus in Bulgaria, contributions have risen from between 5 and 15 per cent of wages in 1971 to 30 per cent today. In Poland they have increased from 15.5 per cent in 1971 to 25 per cent in 1981.

Removal of the ceiling on contributions

The fixing of an upper limit–or ceiling–for the amount of the earnings on which contributions are paid, which is generally linked to the establishment of a similar limit for the calculation of cash benefits–appears to be a survival of the ceiling for coverage characteristic of the early German insurance schemes, which has been retained only in the case of sickness insurance in the Netherlands. The existence of a ceiling for contributions is increasingly contested: the removal of such a ceiling would increase the yield produced by contributions; it would also facilitate the collection of funds by simplifying procedures and would reinforce the redistributive effect of social security. In the post-war years, most social security systems incorporated a ceiling for contributions. Pension systems in Italy, Switzerland and the USSR were practically the only exceptions. Since that time, however, an increasing number of countries have ceased to apply a ceiling and have levied contributions on the entire wages bill, irrespective of any upper limit. This occurred first of all in the socialist countries as a whole (with the exception of the German Democratic Republic) and Finland. The trend towards the removal of the ceiling developed further in the 1970s: in Norway (for employers' contributions first and subsequently for workers' contributions), in Portugal and Sweden. The ceiling has been removed in many branches in Belgium and is now retained only for the purposes of unemployment and invalidity benefits as well as employees' pensions, and even there it has been raised considerably, so that only 4.25 per cent of wages are above it (the ceiling will be removed completely in 1983, under the Law of 29 June 1981). In France, where the ceiling remains relatively low (29 per cent of wage earners earn more than the ceiling), an attempt to remove it in the family benefits branch proved unsuccessful in 1958 (the measure introduced for this purpose by an ordinance dated 30 December 1958 was revoked a few weeks later by another dated 4 February 1959); but in 1967 a measure for the partial removal of the ceiling for sickness insurance was introduced and has since been gradually extended so that now little more than half of the sickness insurance contribution is based on a worker's total earnings. The question whether wages above a certain level should continue to be exempt is also being raised with some insistence in other countries such as the Netherlands.

Recourse to supplementary financing methods

Recourse to other financing methods may stem from a desire to modify, for various reasons, the sharing of social security costs, a subject which will be discussed below. Although it is not always easy to make a clear-cut distinction, the search for supplementary financing may also become indispensable simply in order to cover the costs themselves if a reduction in social security expenditure has proved impossible. Attempts to increase the yield from regular financing sources may well come up against physical or psychological limitations. Besides, such limitations do not apply only to payroll contributions: for example, in Denmark, where the social security system is financed above all from budgetary sources and where the source of the financing is also considered to be a matter of secondary importance, a psychological limit to taxation is believed to exist, and this could well result in greater recourse to contributions in the future. In that case, it may be necessary to diversify resources for them to be increased. In addition, economic policy considerations may militate against increasing the yield of traditional sources of financing.

The difficulties involved in balancing resources and expenditure may initially force governments into making more use of previously established safety procedures. In the legislation of a number of countries provision is made for any possible deficit to be covered by the state budget: this is the case in Austria (pensions and unemployment insurance), Belgium (unemployment insurance), Bulgaria, the German Democratic Republic, the Federal Republic of Germany (unemployment insurance), Greece (pension and sickness insurance), Hungary, Luxembourg (pensions and family benefits), Romania, and the USSR. Rising social security costs lead to greater recourse to this kind of financing. Thus, in the German Democratic Republic, credits from the state budget for social security expenditure represented 35.6 per cent of other resources in 1971 and 44.6 per cent in 1979.

It is above all the introduction or development of social security schemes for non-employed persons which has made it necessary to turn to new sources of financing, since often the full costs of the scheme cannot be borne solely by contributions from the insured persons. In Poland, the old-age fund for agricultural workers which was set up in 1977 was intended to be financed essentially by contributions levied upon the workers concerned and calculated on the value of their holdings, and only in case of necessity by any funding from the state budget; however, the state contribution is larger than the yield of the workers' contributions (more than 80 per cent of the expenses of the fund in 1981). In Finland, the earnings-related pension scheme for self-employed persons was designed to be financed exclusively from contributions from the latter, but since 1978, the State has had to make contributions from the national budget. In France, the social benefits budget for agricultural workers is financed to a much greater extent by specific taxes on agricultural products, fats and alcohol or by subsidies from the state budget or the general social security scheme for wage earners, than by payroll contributions.

Under the pressure of circumstances, it has sometimes proved necessary to turn every means to account to overcome financial difficulties. In Belgium, for example, in addition to direct budgetary aid, recourse has been had in recent years to loans and special taxes (supplementary tax on automobile insurance premiums, revenue from duty on tobacco). Special taxes have also been levied in France (motor car insurance premiums), specific taxation has been imposed (on large incomes) and older workers and persons who are not economically active have been made to contribute (suppression of the exemption from contributions of workers over the age of 65, introduction of a contribution levied on pension benefits, guaranteed income security and unemployment compensation).

Sometimes, when these additional measures are financed from the state budget, the strain on the public finances becomes too great and recourse must again be had to increased contributions. Thus, in Belgium, although the State pays the contributions for unemployed persons, such payments constitute an increasingly heavy burden which will probably have to be financed in future by a readjustment of contributions. The need to make constant increases in these social levies can result in a difficult and precarious seesaw relationship between the various possible sources and methods of financing.

Development of the structure of social levies

As was seen in the first part of this document, the structure of social levies as reflected in the nature and sources of revenue in the various national systems was conditioned first of all by historical factors. Although this structure has remained virtually the same over the past 30 years, or has changed only slightly in some countries, significant developments have occurred in a number of other countries as the volume of social levies as a whole has risen–a subject which has just been examined–and under the impact of an aggregate of political, economic, social or technical factors. The trend of these developments has varied in different countries. Although in a number of cases the structure of financing is today very different from what it was when social security first appeared, taking the industrialised countries as a whole, it still features as many contrasts as ever, in both the respective volume of payroll contributions, tax revenue, and other resources and the sharing of costs between employers and insured persons.

Payroll contributions, tax receipts or other resources

Variations in the respective shares of contributions, taxes, income from capital and other sources in social security financing differ from one country to another. For example the relative importance of contributions increases or remains unchanged in a number of the countries considered, while it declines in others. The main trend, however, seems to be towards an increase or stabilisation in the share of payroll contributions. In several countries, the rise in financing from this source has been very marked: it has almost doubled in Ireland, increased by more than 50 per cent in Malta and Sweden and by about 25 per cent in Finland and Norway. The opposite trend can, however, be noted in other countries, particularly in Denmark, as well as in Iceland, Israel and Japan and, to a considerably lesser extent, in Austria, the Netherlands and Turkey. In several planned economy countries, particularly the USSR,[16] the relative size of contributions is also tending to decline; nevertheless, it is more difficult in these countries to distinguish between employers' contributions and revenue from taxation since the greater part of the latter also comes from the enterprises, although calculated on a different basis.

German social insurance financing methods still exert a very considerable influence: payroll contributions are globally the predominant source of social security financing in the large majority of industrialised countries. They cover at least three-fourths of the total expenditure in 15 of these countries (Austria, Finland, France, the Federal Republic of Germany, Italy, the Netherlands, Norway, Poland, Portugal, Romania, Spain, Turkey, the United Kingdom, the United States, Yugoslavia) and more than 60 per cent in a number of others (Belgium, Bulgaria, Greece, Hungary, Japan, Luxembourg, Sweden, Switzerland).[17] Financing from contributions is of only minor importance in Ireland (although the share is developing rapidly there), Australia, Canada, in a few socialist countries–Czechoslovakia, USSR–and above all in Denmark and New Zealand (less than 5 per cent of revenue).

Correspondingly, the relative importance of the share financed by revenue from taxation has increased in only a small number of countries, in particular in Denmark, where it is now higher than 90 per cent, Austria, Israel, the Netherlands, and Switzerland. However, in all four countries, as in most of the industrialised countries, taxes or levies still account for only less than one-third–and often much less–of the total cost of social security.

This appraisal is doubtless only very general, and in the legislation of a large number of countries financing methods may be different, according to the branch and the persons covered, and the methods themselves may change. Thus, as will be seen in the third part of this document, whilst financing from payroll contributions is still by far the most frequently used method for covering replacement cash benefits, there is a very marked tendency towards increasing the share of taxes for the financing of family benefits, health care and basic pensions. In spite of this tendency the ratio of contributions to total social security resources is often maintained or increased. For example, in the Federal Republic of Germany, this component remained virtually unchanged between 1960 (70.2 per cent) and 1977 (77.9 per cent), although the cost of financing family benefits was transferred during this period from the employers to the public authorities. This can be explained to a significant extent by the respective evolution of the financial cost of each branch. In particular, the volume and the cost of pensions proportional to income from employment, which are generally financed by contributions, are becoming every day greater.

It is in any case remarkable that payroll contributions today finance a large part of social security expenditure in countries where the intervention of the public authorities had traditionally predominated (Finland, Ireland, Malta, Norway, Sweden, the United Kingdom). In Sweden, the transfer to employers' contributions of costs previously borne by the State or local communities deserves special mention. Before 1974, the public authorities contributed 70 per cent of the cost of universal pensions and 34 per cent of that of sickness insurance: today, this share has declined to 43 per cent and 15 per cent, respectively. The State has also transferred to employers' contributions two-fifths of the costs which it previously financed for unemployment insurance and two-thirds of the costs for unemployment assistance. The gradual withdrawal of the public authorities from social security financing is also very evident in Finland: in 1971, contributions from the State and local communities to the financing of basic pensions was reduced by almost half. In the same way, in the United Kingdom insured persons' contributions were raised in 1981 so as to reduce the burden on the Treasury.

The development of the relative size of contributions and subsidies from the public authorities is not only the result of financing needs or the expression of a desire to restructure social security levies so as to diversify them and redistribute the financial burden–whether by a gradual withdrawal of the State from financing as in the examples mentioned above or, on the contrary, by greater state intervention–but is also conditioned in particular by the state of the public finances. The recent history of the old-age and survivors' pensions scheme in Switzerland is an example.

The contribution of the Federal Government and the cantons to the financing of the scheme covered 20 per cent of its cost in 1974 and was expected to reach 25 per cent by 1978. In fact, as a result of the recession and budgetary difficulties, the contribution was on the contrary reduced to 14 per cent in 1975.[18] In the Netherlands, because of the economic crisis, state participation increased. The severe budgetary deficits from 1980 onwards have led to a reduction of this participation (cancellation of the contribution to unemployment insurance, in July 1981).

In the majority of cases, the contribution from the public authorities takes the form of a subsidy from the general budget (of the State or the local communities, as the case may be). Despite the recent trend towards the greater use of earmarked taxes noted above, the latter play only a minor role in such financing. The form of the financial contribution from the public authorities continues to vary considerably according to the country, branch and period. There has been a significant development of the public financing of either the entire expenditure of one or several branches or of a specific class of benefits, in particular basic pensions (see the third part of this report) or benefits granted to certain categories of persons (disabled persons in the Netherlands, family benefits for small-scale farmers in Switzerland). The same is true of benefits granted subject to a means test, the cost of which is covered wholly or in part by the State in Austria, in Belgium (family benefits and pensions), Canada, Finland, Ireland, Italy, Portugal, Switzerland (pensions), the United Kingdom and the United States. As pointed out above, the legislation of many countries makes provision for the coverage of any deficit or, as in Czechoslovakia, of the difference between expenditure and the other resources of the social security budget. The rise in unemployment has led the public authorities to assume responsibility for the social security contributions of unemployed persons, for example, in Belgium and in the Federal Republic of Germany. (In the Netherlands, the Government pays the contributions of workers with low incomes.) In countries which have several occupational insurance schemes, as in France, demographic structure has in some cases made it necessary for the State to provide subsidies. The other traditional forms of participation by the public authorities still survive although they have fared in differing ways. Whilst the coverage of administrative costs, either in whole or in part, seems to exist today only in Finland, Japan and Luxembourg for unemployment benefit, fairly widespread use is still made of public participation calculated as a percentage of other contributions or wages (Cyprus, miners' scheme in France, Israel, Malta, Norway; unemployment insurance in the Netherlands), subsidies which cover a certain proportion of expenditure (Iceland, Japan, Sweden, the United Kingdom), subsidies which are calculated on the basis of the number of insured persons (family benefits scheme in Austria, pensions scheme in Italy) or lump-sum subsidies (pension insurance in the Federal Republic of Germany, Spain).

In most industrialised countries, payroll contributions coupled with funds from the public authorities account for almost 90 per cent of total social security resources. The other receipts–mainly income from capital–are thus generally of only very limited importance. This can be easily explained by the fact that many countries in the post-war years abandoned financing by funding in favour of a pay-as-you-go system, so that many

18

national social security systems maintain only a small reserve fund, including reserves for the pensions branch. However, in a few countries where some degree of financing by funding has been retained, and especially in those countries where pensions schemes are relatively new, such as Canada, Israel, Japan and Sweden, the accumulation of reserves has become sufficiently large for income from capital to make a significant contribution to social security financing. In Sweden, for example, which introduced an earnings-related pensions scheme in 1959, the organisation of which was designed to produce a large accumulation of funds, income from investments accounted for 12.4 per cent of social security financing in 1977 and social security has become the major source of capital formation in the country.[19]

Employers' quotas or insured persons' contributions

It will be recalled that when social security was first introduced, a tendency was already developing towards the reduction, in comparison with the pre-war period, of the relative contribution charge imposed on wage earners. This tendency has been generally confirmed and reinforced over the past 30 years.

First of all, the number of countries which have abolished all forms of workers' contributions and transferred at least part of the corresponding costs to employers has increased. Thus most of the socialist countries have followed the example of the USSR: Albania, Bulgaria, Czechoslovakia, Romania (except for the financing of voluntary pensions) and, more recently, Poland, where workers' contributions, which had been abolished at the end of the Second World War and re-established in 1968, have once again since 1972 been progressively suppressed in the socialised sector (but not in the non-socialised sector). In addition, two Nordic countries have followed the same course, Iceland (except for sickness insurance) and Sweden (except for unemployment insurance).

Some branches are traditionally financed without workers' contributions and this situation has generally remained unchanged. Thus the cost of employment injury benefits is still borne entirely by employers, with the exception of, first, the Netherlands, where these benefits are incorporated in the other social security branches for which wage earners pay contributions and secondly, those countries which have adopted a unified system of financing incorporating workers' contributions–Cyprus, Malta, the United Kingdom–(to which may be added the special case of wage earners over the age of 65 in Ireland who must pay contributions for the employment injuries branch). Family benefits continue to be financed by employers and/or the public authorities, except in Greece where financing is provided by equal contributions from employers and wage earners.

In the other branches which are financed in the large majority of countries and social security schemes by contributions from both workers and employers (and/or the public authorities)–namely, pensions, sickness and maternity benefits as well as unemployment–it can be seen that globally the employers' contributions have everywhere tended to rise more than those of workers. Thus in a number of countries where in 1950 insured persons' contributions to these three branches taken together were greater than those of employers (Belgium, Luxembourg, Norway, the United Kingdom) or equal to the latter (Austria, Federal Republic of Germany, Ireland (except for women wage earners), Czechoslovakia, Turkey), such contributions are now less than those of employers or have been suppressed. The global worker's contribution is at present nowhere higher than that of the employer, with the exception of the Netherlands–and also Yugoslavia, where social security is financed essentially by charges imposed on the portion of enterprise resources earmarked for individual incomes, that is to say in reality by contributions levied on the worker (but this is a specific system established within the framework of self-management); and only a minority of countries have retained a system based on equal contributions, in particular Cyprus, the Federal Republic of Germany, Malta, Switzerland, the United States (for pensions) and, if unemployment insurance is excluded, Brazil, Canada, Japan and Luxembourg. In the large majority of industrialised countries, workers' contributions are now less than those of employers and amount to only half, or even less, of those of employers in such countries as Finland, France, Greece, Ireland, Israel, Italy (7.80 per cent against 37.20 per cent in industrial enterprises employing more than 50 wage earners), Norway, Portugal, Spain or the United Kingdom.

The trend towards the reduction of contributions by insured persons appears to be undeniable. In recent years, however, in particular under the impact of the economic crisis and for fear of putting too great a financial burden on enterprises, the tendency in several countries has been to increase workers' contributions. The Netherlands had already opened up this way by imposing on wage earners most of the financing for the old-age pensions, survivors' and invalidity benefits (17.7 per cent for wage earners against 10.35 per cent for employers). On several occasions France has increased workers' contributions more than employers' contributions by removing the ceiling for sickness insurance contributions (although employers' contributions are still partially subject to a ceiling), increasing the scale of these contributions on a temporary basis, and making contributions to the new widows' insurance scheme applicable only to wage earners . . .[20] In the United Kingdom, the contributions of wage earners to the national insurance scheme were increased by 1 per cent from 1 April 1981.

The question of the apportionment of social security costs between employers and wage earners does not of course arise in the case of self-employed persons, whose social protection has been extended considerably in the industrialised countries over the past 30 years. Another question which does, however, arise as regards the financing of the social security schemes for this category is whether self-employed workers should contribute at the same rates as employers and wage earners taken together or whether they should be granted more favourable arrangements, supplementary financing being provided in various ways through a national solidarity contribution. The answer to this question varies from country to country and may also depend upon the nature of the work involved (handicrafts, agricultural work, etc.). In a number of countries contributions from self-employed workers are calculated on the basis of income from employment and are equal or almost equal to the combined contributions of employers and wage earners. This is the case, for example, in Canada (pensions scheme), Cyprus, the Federal Republic of Germany, Israel, Portugal, Switzerland (old-age pensions and disability benefit).

In other countries, self-employed workers are required to pay a much lower contribution: in Norway, this amounts to 9.9 per cent of the pensionable income whereas the combined contributions of employers and wage earners are equivalent to 21.5 per cent; in the United States, the rate is 9.3 per cent against 13.4 per cent. Even in those countries where workers' contributions have been abolished, self-employed workers generally have to continue to participate in financing. In Poland, for example, self-employed agricultural workers pay contributions which are levied on the same basis as the other taxes to which they are liable (land tax and income tax); however, as noted above, most of the cost of the scheme is financed by the State. In Sweden, self-employed workers are also obliged to pay contributions calculated on the basis of income, at a rate identical to that of employers for universal pensions schemes, earnings-related pensions and sickness insurance. The situation in Bulgaria is the same.

Reorganisation of financing techniques

Although payroll contributions are still by far the most commonly used method of financing social security schemes, significant developments have taken place since the end of the war in the techniques of calculating contributions. These trends, already nascent during the early social security period, have developed further since then. Three of them deserve special consideration: the progressive suppression of the risk factor in the calculation of insurance contributions or premiums, the extension of wage- or earnings-related contributions and the recourse to taxation techniques.

Discontinuance of insurance-based differential contribution rates

The search for a certain balance between the size of the insurance premium and the probable cost of benefits, taking account of the risk class of the insured person, is a basic characteristic of the insurance principle. In the case of social insurance, this concern has not completely disappeared despite the fact that it conflicts with the social objectives of schemes. Social security has progressively tended to abandon any such remaining differential contribution rates, but the process seems to be much more general when the elements taken into consideration concern the personal situation of the insured person than when they involve occupational hazards.

The most important risk elements concerning an insured person are age, sex, and family situation (on account of the coverage of dependent persons). In 1950, contribution rates in a number of countries took account of these factors. In Denmark, contributions to the invalidity insurance scheme were lower for persons insured before the age of 21. In Iceland, Ireland, the Netherlands and the United Kingdom, contributions in all or some of the branches were higher for men than for women and for adults than for young persons. On the other hand, in Iceland, a heavier burden was placed on married than on single persons. Although such differentiations have now largely disappeared, it may be noted that in Malta contributions of young persons under the age of 18 are still lower than those of adults and, in Japan, women's contributions to pension schemes are fixed at a lower rate than those of men.

It was previously common practice almost everywhere to rate contributions for the occupational injuries and diseases branch on the basis of the risks involved in the enterprise or sector of activity concerned. The principle still applies in most countries, although it is tending to be replaced by fixed contributions at a flat rate irrespective of the risk involved in the enterprise or sector in a growing number of countries which have decided to move towards the pooling of risks in respect of employment injuries, in line with the other branches of social security.[21] Since the early days of social security, a uniform rate of contributions has been progressively adopted, first of all in countries with a single financing system (socialist countries –except the German Democratic Republic, where contributions continue to be differentiated on the basis of the risk incurred by the enterprise, Cyprus, Malta, the United Kingdom and more recently, in 1969, Norway), and also in Austria, Ireland, the Netherlands (1966) and Sweden (1972). The trend, however, has gone in the opposite direction in Japan where occupational risks did not originally constitute a separate branch and all contributions in the existing branches were fixed at a uniform rate until 1947 when the situation changed and a system of differential rates was introduced. In the United States also, employers' contributions to unemployment insurance are differentiated having regard to the employment record of the enterprise.[22]

Extension of wage- and earnings-related contributions

There was already a tendency in the early days of social security to move away from the system of fixed uniform contribution rates–in other words, not varying with wages or income–which was reputedly easier to understand and administer, although it was strongly degressive and of low yield in so far as contributions could not be set at a very high level. This trend has since been reinforced, in particular in association with the extension of earnings-related benefits, which were difficult to finance by uniform contribution rates. Thus Iceland (with the exception of workers' contributions to unemployment insurance), Ireland and the United Kingdom (with the exception of inactive persons) and recently Malta (1978) and Cyprus (1980) have replaced this system by one of wage- or earnings-related contributions. Today a system based on uniform contributions is no longer used except, in a few countries, for certain branches or categories of insured persons: for workers' contributions to sickness insurance in Australia (the amount varies according to the State of residence), contributions from self-employed workers in the occupational accidents branch in Austria, employers' contributions in the pensions and unemployment branches and workers' contributions in the invalidity pensions branch in Denmark, workers' contributions in the national pensions branch in Japan and workers' contributions to unemployment insurance in Sweden.

In the same way, the system of assessing contributions on the basis of wage categories to which a fixed contribution rate is applicable is clearly losing ground. Contributions are calculated on this basis only in Spain (12 classes), Greece (22 classes), Japan (36 or 39 classes) and Malta for the self-employed (6 classes).

The great majority of industrialised countries have thus progressively adopted the modern formula of contributions established strictly in accordance with wages or earnings, subject to the existence of a ceiling.

Recourse to taxation techniques

The discontinuance of contributions differentiated according to the risk involved, which is an essential component of the insurance principle, and the extension of wage- or earnings-related contributions are already tending to assimilate payroll contributions to income tax, which is the modern method of levying taxes, in contrast for example to the practice still followed in a number of developing countries of levying a poll tax. This tendency towards the application of similar techniques for the purposes of social security and income tax, whether in connection with the contribution base and method of calculation or with collection, is becoming even more marked in certain countries.

First of all, as regards the contribution base and method of calculation, reference has already been made to the discontinuance by a number of countries of any ceiling on the wages which are taken into account for the purposes of determining contributions, that is to say the replacement of a system of degressive contributions by one of contributions which are proportional to global earnings. Several Nordic countries have adopted the former New Zealand system of calculating contributions from insured persons, either wholly or in part, in proportion to the income liable to national or local taxation. This is the case in Iceland for sickness insurance contributions, in Denmark for the universal pensions scheme, and in Finland for sickness insurance contributions and universal pensions. In Norway, a contribution levied on the whole taxable income most of which is used to finance medical care is combined with a contribution levied on income from employment applicable to both wage earners and self-employed

23

workers. In the Netherlands, self-employed workers' contributions to the family benefits scheme are proportional to net income. In Sweden, prior to 1974, contributions from insured persons who participated in the financing of sickness insurance were also proportional to taxable income. A more pronounced trend is perhaps emerging in Hungary where contribution rates, like income tax rates in all industrialised countries, are structured progressively. However, this example has not yet been followed by other countries.

As regards the collection of contributions, several countries, such as France, are tending to co-ordinate control of the income tax and contribution bases. Other countries, especially Malta, the Netherlands, Norway, Sweden and the United States, have gone much further towards simplifying and unifying their administrative procedures by making the taxation authorities responsible for the collection of social security contributions.

CURRENT TRENDS

It can be seen from the above that social security financing systems are, on the whole, quite different today from what they were when social security first made its appearance; however, development has by no means been the same everywhere and has not been so pronounced, or followed the same lines, in all the industrialised countries. All national social protection systems have undoubtedly made use of increasingly higher social charges–sometimes the increases have been very steep–but this has not always involved any reorganisation of financing–or the same sort of reorganisation–or brought about major changes in the techniques used. Whilst some countries, such as Sweden or, in a different way, Yugoslavia, have radically transformed their system for the financing of social benefits, other countries, such as the Federal Republic of Germany or the United States have been much more conservative in this respect.

Despite the concern felt by governments, it seems unavoidable that social security expenditure will continue to rise, perhaps at a slower rate, for some time to come, especially in the light of demographic trends and the economic outlook. The need to adapt the level of resources to that of expenditure will continue to pose serious problems and is likely to affect the methods and techniques of social charges as the serious difficulties resulting from the economic crisis inter alia militate for radical reform. The question of the inadequacy of the traditional forms of financing and the need to find alternative methods has been under discussion for several years: it is the subject of frequent debate and has been examined in numerous studies and reports. Certain radical reform proposals (for example, the use of added value as the basis for charges) have been repeatedly put forward [23] but scarcely any notice has been taken of them so far in national legislation. Numerous measures, most of which have been restricted to specific points, have been adopted under the pressure of circumstances in recent years (the so-called "elastoplast policy", or piecemeal reform).[24] Such an approach may be viewed as evidence of rigid opposition to structural reform: however, it may also be a sign of a gradual drift towards progressive change. If this is the case, in such a group of widely different measures it is difficult–and doubtless premature–to seek to identify all the basic new tendencies which herald future changes. It is nevertheless possible to try to discern some of the trends which seem destined to take shape in the years to come, at least in a fairly large number of industrialised countries.

Thus, if analysis is restricted to a relatively general level, three major tendencies seem likely to develop in the future: greater adaptation of financing methods to the operational requirements of the economy, the establishment of a more logical relationship between financing methods and techniques and the aims and functions of social security, and closer harmonisation of social security charges and the general taxation system.

Contributions and economic exigencies

The use of social security financing as an instrument of economic intervention is no novelty. Long before the war, in the USSR, the differentiation of contribution rates according to the enterprise was based not only on the risk involved or the noxiousness of the work, but also closely coordinated with current economic policy: the highest rate was imposed on all private employers, with reductions in the normal rate granted on account of certain economic factors, for example for work on the construction of new buildings.[25] At the beginning of the social security period, the British Act of 1 August 1946 allowed for variation of the contribution rate in accordance with the economic situation "with a view to maintaining a stable level of employment".[26] It may also be added that Convention No. 102 stipulates that social security financing methods must take into account the economic situation of the country concerned.

It was, however, during the past decade–as a result of the problem of constant increases in the size of social charges, coupled with stagnation or low growth of GDP (which is ultimately the general base for such contributions)–that considerable interest developed in the choice of financing methods and their impact on the national economy. Since social charges are not inert factors having no effect on the national economy (any kind of levy on a flow of production is an economic factor), it is being increasingly maintained that financing methods should try to neutralise the negative effects which they may exert, particularly at their present high levels, on various sectors of the economy, or even be designed in such a way as to make social security financing an instrument of economic policy.

Much attention has been given in this respect to the problem of employment. In countries where financing depends mainly on employers' contributions, the search for other financing methods is above all dictated by a desire to reduce the pernicious effects on employment of social charges borne by enterprises. The relation between social security financing and employment is discussed in another chapter. This document is concerned only with changes in financing methods which may have been brought about by a concern to avoid measures discouraging employment and to identify possible future trends. It will be seen moreover–and this needs stressing from the outset–that great prudence has been shown in this respect, in particular owing to the multiple uncertainties that persist concerning the real impact of the various financing methods on employment, as on other variables in the economy.[27]

This prudence is particularly evident when a change in financing methods or a change in the contribution base are involved. The replacement of wages by added value as a contribution base or the replacement of all or part of the contributions by a supplementary tax on added value have been advocated in various countries for several years, in particular in Belgium, France and the Netherlands (although they were rejected in the United States by the National Commission on Social Security, which had recommended that contributions should be supplemented from the proceeds of general taxation,[28] before the National Commission on the reform of social security, set up in 1981, ruled out any direct recourse to public funds); so far, however, these proposals have only been implemented in Argentina, Belgium and Uruguay. In Argentina, the Act of 30 September 1980 abolished the employers' contribution to the pensions scheme and replaced it by a payment from public funds, the additional burden being met by an increase in value added tax (see Chapter 4). In Belgium, the Act of 29 June 1981 introduced a minor degree of substitution using similar indirect methods: workers' contributions were reduced by 6.17 points and the shortfall in receipts was made up by a subsidy from the state budget, the additional burden on public funds being covered by an increase in value added tax.

No measures have been taken to finance social security by taxing factors of production other than labour, a policy that has been advocated as a means of promoting employment.[29] On the other hand, in some countries, as noted above, part of the social costs of enterprises have been taken over by public funds in order to stimulate employment, improve international competitivity or curb price rises, in case of cost-induced inflation (although the positive effects of these measures are not universally recognised).[30] This tendency is exemplified by recent legislation in Italy, which provides for a part of the employers' contribution to sickness insurance to be taken over by public funds in connection with the introduction of a national health service.

The fixing of employers' contribution rates for each enterprise for reasons of economic policy, in particular to favour the labour factor and no longer in application of insurance principles, is a new trend (if exception is made of the earlier USSR experiment) which seems to be spreading. Thus in Finland, the employers' contribution rate to the basic pensions system has varied since 1973 in accordance with the capital-intensive nature of the enterprise measured in terms of the relation between the depreciation of the capital used for the production process and the total wage bill (three different rates have thus been established). In Norway, employers' contributions have been divided since 1975 into three differentiated rates according to the area of regional development, the lowest being reserved for those areas where investment subsidies are highest (in 1981 the number of rates was increased to four); this differential is thus a component of a national development policy which is designed in particular to encourage firms to move to areas with a high rate of unemployment. (Measures designed to use social security financing as a means of encouraging the development of certain regions of the country have also been introduced in Yugoslavia, where the State, although it does not generally participate in this financing, grants subsidies to social security bodies in the least-developed districts, and also in Italy, where reduced contribution rates are granted to enterprises in the Mezzogiorno.) In other countries, employers' contributions have been reduced or abolished, in most cases temporarily, for certain categories of workers, in particular young persons. This was the case, for example, in Belgium in 1977 and 1978 for young persons engaged by enterprises and, in 1979, for apprentices in small firms. Similar provisions were adopted in France under the National Employment Pacts and others were introduced under the 1981 corrective finance Act; in Italy also the same policy was applied to enterprises taking on apprentices with job-training contracts.

The removal of the ceiling on contributions is another device calculated to promote employment, particularly since the existence of a ceiling encourages recourse to overtime at the expense of the recruitment of new workers. As was seen in the preceding section, there is a very marked tendency towards abolishing any kind of ceiling in calculating contributions and there is every probability that this trend, which serves to neutralise one of the most pernicious effects of traditional contribution mechanisms, will continue.

Adaptation of financing methods to the aims and functions of social security

One of the virtues of financing social insurance schemes by contributions lies in the "transparent" nature of such a system: there is a clear, reasonable and therefore comprehensible relation between the contributions paid and the benefits received which makes it easier to accept the burden of such contributions. The trend towards the generalisation of social security and the dissociation of social protection from occupational activity, the development of non-contributory benefits and selectivity as well as the diversification of resources under the pressure of circumstances has to a large extent clouded this transparency. The continuance of this process, coupled particularly with the need to find more and more supplementary resources to cope with rising costs, is in a number of cases making it even more difficult to see the relationship between financing methods on the one hand and the nature of the benefits or the objectives and functions of the social protection systems on the other, although such developments are also making it increasingly desirable to give social security systems new coherence. This concern is reflected in two different tendencies in national legislation.

The first of these tendencies is the development of unified financing systems, which were first introduced (at least partially) in the USSR at the beginning of the 1920s. The total resources of the system are used to cover the expenditure of all the branches of the scheme taken together, no particular resource being allocated to any particular branch, in compliance with the principle of the non-allocation of receipts which governs public finances, where generally speaking the receipts from any one tax are not reserved for any specific budgetary item.

Under this system, financing is generally based on a combination of various resources and the only problem which arises is how best to apportion funds so as to obtain the most equitable distribution of charges in line with the financial, economic, political and administrative priorities at any given moment. A number of national legislations have thus partially or completely unified the financing of their social security systems: all the countries of Eastern Europe with the exception of Yugoslavia, Cyprus, Malta, New Zealand, Norway and the United Kingdom. In most cases, such global financing does not apply to medical care or family benefits, which are financed directly by the national budget. For the time being, movement in this direction seems to have come to a halt–in the past 20 years, only Norway followed this trend, when it expanded its national insurance scheme–although in Sweden there seems perhaps to be a tendency towards unified financing on the basis of employers' contributions. In Norway, the unified system does not in any case exclude some allocation of receipts: insured persons' contributions which are levied on the total taxable income (added, as already stated, to another contribution paid by insured persons and employers and based on income from employment) are for the most part allocated to the financing of medical care.

Another tendency follows up an idea originally put forward by Beveridge (financing the national health service and family benefits from the budget and cash benefits from payroll contributions) which is now very often developed to mean: the nature of receipts must be adapted to that of expenditure. Benefits which are designed to guarantee occupational income should be financed by a contribution levied on this income (the traditional payroll tax), whilst benefits designed to guarantee minimum social standards (basic pensions, family benefits) or health care benefits should be covered by a national solidarity effort (financing from the public budget).[31] The desirability of earmarking funds for the various branches of social security is, however, criticised by some writers who believe that the distinction between contributions and taxes is perhaps of only limited significance in as far as the real effects of both forms of levies may in the end not be very different.[32]

Be that as it may, there is nevertheless a fairly marked tendency to use public funds to finance all or most of the cash benefits designed to satisfy minimum social standards, in so far as these benefits are granted to all or almost all of the population. Thus the public authorities now finance the whole branch of family benefits in many countries which have established statutory or *de facto* universal schemes: Australia, Canada, Denmark, the German Democratic Republic, the Federal Republic of Germany, Iceland, Ireland, New Zealand, Norway, Romania, the United Kingdom and the USSR. The public authorities finance some of the costs of certain benefits (maternity grants or benefits subject to a means test) in Belgium, Finland and Luxembourg. On the other hand, in Austria, France, Israel and the Netherlands, where family benefits are also granted to the whole population, financing is still, at least in part, provided by employers' contributions (although, as stated above, the financing of family benefits out of taxes is envisaged in France). Universal pensions schemes or benefits subject to a means test, designed to guarantee a minimum income for the aged are also entirely or for the most part financed by public funds in a number of countries: Australia, Austria, Belgium, Canada, Denmark, Iceland, Italy, Luxembourg, New Zealand, but in other countries, such as Finland (where total financing by the State applies only to universal survivors' pensions schemes), France, Japan or Sweden, although payroll contributions are supplemented by financing from the public authorities, the latter remains of only secondary importance. As regards medical care, financing from public funds plays a major role in only a limited number of schemes: those of the countries of Eastern Europe (except the German Democratic Republic), Australia, Canada, Denmark, Iceland, Ireland, New Zealand and the United Kingdom. In Australia and Iceland, it is supplemented by a contribution from the insured person, which is a fixed amount in the Australian scheme and calculated in proportion to taxable income in the Icelandic scheme.

Branches providing replacement income are still largely financed by payroll contributions–levied only on employers for employment injury benefits, with a double contribution, except in a few cases, for earnings-related pensions and unemployment, health and maternity benefits–although there is a tendency, as yet not very marked, in the legislation of a growing number of countries to make use, in very different forms, of assistance from the public authorities, particularly for the unemployment branch.

Closer harmonisation of the social security system and the tax system

Social charges have traditionally enjoyed greater autonomy than taxation; this situation, however, is now being substantially modified and there is every reason to believe that the trend towards integration or at least closer harmonisation between the two systems will develop further in the coming years.

It can be seen, first, that increasing account is being taken of compulsory charges as a whole–whether in the form of contributions or income tax–when the tax burden is being evaluated, in particular for the purpose of making international comparisons.[33] In the Netherlands, for example, although the contributions burden and the tax burden are technically separate, they are considered as a single "collective burden" for the purposes of economic planning.[34] In the same way, at the level of the enterprise, less and less distinction is made between taxes and social charges.

At the institutional decision-making level, there is an evident movement in several countries towards harmonising the two categories of charges. In Norway, for example, Parliament fixes both the social security contribution rates and the tax rates and it intervenes in the approval of the social security budget. In France, a social security audit committee was created in 1979, to provide Parliament with more information on the financial problems of social security.

As was seen in the second part of this chapter, there is a very marked trend towards harmonising social contribution techniques and taxation techniques, particularly as regards the base and calculation of contributions. Also noteworthy in this respect is the importance given in financing reform projects to formulas which have been successfully tested in general taxation, such as the value added tax. Furthermore, there is a tendency for systems of social charges to acquire various characteristics typical of modern tax systems, in particular in becoming increasingly elaborate and complex, especially as they pursue, at the economic and social levels, a policy of simultaneous neutrality and interventionism. Social charges are being increasingly considered as taxes.[35]

In as far as both these systems of charges are now of comparable importance and have similar characteristics, a problem being more and more frequently raised in the industrialised countries is whether they are compatible, in respect of both the improvement of the apportionment of the global burden and the harmonisation of their impact on the economy.

Notes

[1] Hubert Korkisch: "The financial resources of social insurance", in *International Labour Review* (Geneva, ILO), Dec. 1924, pp. 909-934.

[2] Memorandum to the German Government Invalidity Insurance Bill, in *Stenographische Berichte über die Verhandlungen des Reichstages 1888-1889*, Vol. 4, p. 58, quoted by Korkisch, op. cit., p. 911.

[3] It should be noted, however, that several pioneers of modern social security had envisaged similar sources of financing. Thus in Brussels, Bosschaert advocated the institution of mutual aid funds to be financed by employers' contributions and in France, Count de Boulainvilliers intended that the "common bursary" or compulsory insurance scheme which he recommended would be financed by part of the wages of beneficiaries. See J. P. Gutton: *La société et les pauvres en Europe* (Paris, 1974), pp. 165 and 170.

[4] See ILO: *General problems of social insurance*, Studies and Reports, Series M, No. 1 (Geneva, 1925), pp. 43-62, and idem: *The financing of social security*, Report III, First European Regional Conference of the ILO, 1955 (Geneva, 1954).

[5] See the report of the Committee on the general problems of social insurance, International Labour Conference, 7th Session, Geneva, 1925, and the resolution adopted by the Conference on this matter in idem: *Record of Proceedings* (Geneva, ILO, 1925), Vol. II, pp. 807-815 and 832-834.

[6] idem: *General problems of social insurance*, op. cit., pp. 43-76 and pp. 127-129; idem: *Compulsory sickness insurance*, Studies and Reports, Series M, No. 6 (Geneva, 1927), pp. 19-23 and pp. 405-552; idem: *Compulsory pension insurance*, Studies and Reports, Series M, No. 10 (Geneva, 1933), pp. 13-15 and pp. 441-564; idem: *Approaches to social security: An international survey*, Studies and Reports, Series M, No. 18 (Montreal, 1942, pp. 65-69).

[7] idem: *General problems of social insurance*, op. cit., p. 61.

[8] idem: *Non-contributory pensions*, Studies and Reports, Series M, No. 9 (Geneva, 1933), p. 103.

[9] ibid., p. 15.

[10] *Social insurance and allied services*. Report by Sir William Beveridge (London, HM Stationery Office; New York, Macmillan, 1942).

[11] P. Laroque: "From social insurance to social security: Evolution in France", in *International Labour Review*, June 1948, p. 570.

[12] "Post-war trends in social security", in *International Labour Review*, June 1949 and Sep. 1949, p. 32.

[13] ILO: *The cost of social security*, op. cit.

[14] See in this connection "Social security at the crossroads", in *International Labour Review*, Mar.-Apr. 1980, pp. 140-142; Guy Perrin: "La sécurité sociale au passé et au présent", in *Revue française des affaires sociales* (Paris, La documentation française), Jan.-Mar. 1979, p. 127; and Pierre Rosanvallois: *La crise de l'Etat-providence* (Paris, Editions du Seuil, 1981), pp. 17 and 33.

[15] "Post-war trends in social security", op. cit.

[16] V. A. Acharkan and T. A. Simitsina: *Fondy sotcialnogo obespechenia v SSSR* (Moscow, Izdatelstvo Finansy, 1977), p. 27.

[17] ILO: *The cost of social security*, op. cit.

[18] Frank B. McArdle: "Impact of recession on Swiss pension program", in *Social Security Bulletin* (Washington, DC), Apr. 1978; and idem: "Sources of revenue of social security systems in ten industrialised countries", in *Social Security in a Changing World* (Washington, DC, United States Department of Health, Education and Welfare, Sep. 1979), pp. 55-56.

[19] McArdle: "Sources of revenue of social security systems . . .", op. cit., pp. 64-67.

[20] See Yves Saint-Jours: "Imputation aux assurés sociaux du redressement financier de la sécurité sociale", in *Droit social* (Paris), Jan. 1981.

[21] See on this subject A. Zelenka: *The contribution of social security to accident prevention: Influence on prevention of the methods of financing employment injury insurance*, working document for the ILO Meeting of Experts on Occupational Accident Prevention and Compensation (Geneva, 29 January-2 February 1979), document OAPC/1979/D2.

[22] OECD: *Unemployment compensation and related employment policy measures* (Paris, 1979), p. 10.

[23] See for example M. Lhaguenot: "Pour une TVA *bis*", in *Le Monde* (Paris), 9 June 1982.

[24] *Rapport de la Commission protection sociale et famille*. Préparation de huitième plan, 1981-1985 (Paris, La documentation française, July 1980), p. 203.

[25] ILO: *Compulsory pension insurance*, op. cit., pp. 561-562.

[26] idem: "Post-war trends in social security", op. cit., p. 41.

[27] On the interest and limitations of using econometric models to identify these effects, see M. A. Coppini and G. Laina: *Mieux connaître les transferts sociaux par l'utilisation des modèles économétriques* (Geneva, ILO, forthcoming).

[28] *Social security in America's future*. Final report of the National Commission on Social Security (Washington, DC, Mar. 1981).

[29] See for example P. Artus, H. Sterdyniak and P. Villa: "Investissement, emploi et fiscalité", in *Economie et statistique* (Paris, Institut national de la statistique et des études économiques), Nov. 1980, pp. 115-127.

[30] For the Netherlands, see the conclusions of the article by A. F. Bakhoven: "Fiscalisiering van sociale verzekeringspremies", in *Openbare uitgaven*, Feb. 1980. For Italy, see Ministerio del Lavoro e della Previdenza sociale: *La fiscalizzazione degli oneri sociali* (Rome, 1979).

[31] See in particular J. J. Dupeyroux: "Sécurité sociale, adapter la nature des ressources à celle des dépenses", in *Le Monde*, 21 Sep. 1976 and idem: *Droit de la sécurité sociale* (Paris, Dalloz, 8th ed., 1980), pp. 172 and 173; A. Euzéby: "Faut-il fiscaliser la sécurité sociale?", in *Droit social*, May 1978, pp. 181-190 and idem: "Financement de la sécurité sociale et emploi", in *Droit social*, Nov. 1979, pp. 384-395; and Guy Perrin: "A propos du financement de la sécurité sociale", in *Revue belge de sécurité sociale* (Brussels), Oct. 1980.

[32] See for example J. Fournier and N. Questiaux: *Le pouvoir du social* (Paris, Presses universitaires de France, 1979), p. 269: "To confuse matters even more, financiers make use of the concept of national solidarity. They are the first to realise that although the repercussions of both social charges and taxes are complex, their respective impact cannot be clearly distinguished ... Yet scholarly studies are undertaken in an attempt to analyse which expenditure would be more appropriately financed by taxes". See also International Social Security Association: *Methods of financing social security*, General report by John Osborne, Studies and Research, No. 15 (Geneva, 1979), pp. 100-101.

[33] See for example Richard Goode: "Limits to taxation", in *Finance and Development* (Washington, DC, International Monetary Fund and World Bank), Mar. 1980.

[34] Council of Europe: *Financing of social security*, First Report of the Conference of European Ministers Responsible for Social Security (Strasbourg, 1979), p. 9.

[35] See J. H. Petersen: "Financing social security by means of taxation", in ISSA: *Methods of financing social security*, op. cit., pp. 25-60; and P. Laroque, R. A. B. Leaper and M. Pfaff: *Prospects for a European social policy for the next ten years*, prepared for the Council of Europe, document CDAS (79) 28 rev. (Strasbourg, 1980), p. 35, where the authors point out that a contribution from insured persons may be considered as a tax on earnings and a contribution from employers as a tax on the firms.

SOCIAL SECURITY FINANCING AND ECONOMIC GROWTH: A STATISTICAL ANALYSIS *

2

INTRODUCTION

Since the beginning of the fifties, the ILO has conducted, at regular intervals, ten international inquiries on the cost of social security. The results of the sixth inquiry in the series have just been published.[1] The ILO's inquiries aim, in the first instance, at presenting a detailed and uniform statement of the financial operations of social security schemes and, in the second instance, at facilitating international comparisons. In order to measure the importance of social security in the economy of each country, the receipts and expenditures are related to various macro-economic aggregates drawn from national accounts as well as to selected demographic aggregates.

The purpose of this chapter is to provide statistical information to supplement the studies and analyses of trends described in the preceding chapter.

The data provided by the successive ILO inquiries on the cost of social security make it possible to study:

(a) the evolution of social security receipts;

(b) the relationship between the development of social security receipts and of the Gross Domestic Product (GDP) or of the Net Material Product (NMP) in the centrally planned economies;

(c) the distribution of social security receipts by source, and the trends observed in this respect.

The period selected for the study is 1960-77, 1977 being the latest year for which international data on the financial operations of social security are available.

With regard to the scope of the study, the social security systems analysed include social insurance schemes and assimilated schemes such as family allowances schemes, according to the terminology adopted in the ILO inquiries mentioned above. Schemes for public servants and military

---

* Social Security Department of the ILO.

Table 1. Evolution of social security receipts in absolute amounts in OECD countries and European centrally planned economies, 1960-77 (millions of national currency units)

Country	1960	1965	1970	1974	1975	1976	1977
OECD countries							
Australia[1]	758.4	1 140.3	1 757.6	3 520.3	4 966.7	7 615.8	9 573.7
Austria	17 538.0	32 846.0	52 341.0	89 002.0	100 629.0	113 625.0	128 276.0
Belgium[2]	59 830.2	110 219.6	180 957.3	342 037.0	443 707.7	509 195.5	570 025.5
Canada[2]	1 638.6	2 303.7	7 029.0	13 220.8	17 066.9	19 670.8	21 878.5
Denmark[3]	2 410.9	4 638.6	9 695.3	18 718.2	23 744.4	28 811.3	37 375.6
Finland	761.6	1 825.2	3 388.3	7 910.8	10 729.4	13 593.2	16 308.1
France	27 400.4	53 322.8	112 348.0	202 615.5	252 741.5	300 792.3	353 172.1
Germany (Fed. Rep. of)	34 068.0	55 661.0	88 347.0	153 119.0	185 158.0	202 908.0	212 528.0
Greece	530.9	13 479.0	26 422.0	45 507.0	58 031.0	77 702.0	98 987.0
Iceland	33.7	1 390.1	3 528.3	12 865.7	28 237.0	37 203.0	47 776.0
Ireland[4]		53.2	96.2	212.9	371.6	456.5	523.4
Italy	2 122 265.0	4 583 956.0	7 688 062.0	16 723 860.0	18 107 000.0	22 683 000.0	28 291 000.0
Japan[2]	414 959.0	1 144 233.0	3 200 916.0	7 070 040.0	9 818 591.0	12 228 641.0	14 636 173.0
Luxembourg	3 062.3	4 798.4	7 456.1	13 245.6	16 269.8	19 849.4	22 038.1
Netherlands[2]	4 195.5	9 152.2	20 165.1	41 162.0	48 692.4	56 817.0	61 022.8
New Zealand[2]	223.2	259.2	339.4	666.1	770.8	975.0	1 713.5
Norway	2 132.0	3 999.4	9 977.9	20 241.1	23 127.2	25 951.3	27 383.0
Portugal	2 907.1	5 484.5	11 022.6	23 916.2	38 458.1	48 030.9	·
Spain	23 321.0	53 990.1	209 900.0	608 907.5	684 770.0	770 041.5	1 059 643.5
Sweden	4 888.5	12 010.6	24 081.2	44 502.0	50 084.6	61 316.0	71 399.4
Switzerland	2 189.5	3 866.6	7 112.6	14 684.6	15 938.3	17 239.3	17 870.4
Turkey[2]	562.6	1 210.8	3 592.7	11 162.0	16 878.3	24 176.6	34 768.2
United Kingdom[2]	1 172.0	1 742.0	2 945.0	4 945.0	6 529.0	8 334.0	10 288.0
United States[1]	17 423.0	25 894.0	54 740.0	93 339.0	104 548.0	112 308.0	133 345.0
European countries with centrally planned economies							
Bulgaria	362.6[5]	545.8	1 168.9	1 717.5	1 813.3	1 879.5	2 004.3
Czechoslovakia		·	40 965.0	51 366.0	52 605.0	57 165.0	59 124.0
German Democratic Republic			14 394.6	21 091.8	21 827.8	22 721.1	25 075.3
Hungary	13 034.0[5]	18 162.0	30 095.0	50 042.0	58 795.0	66 577.0	72 520.0
Poland	22 563.0			109 019.0	138 041.0	160 915.0	
Romania	5 300.2	8 645.6	15 495.5	23 962.9	25 366.3	29 035.5	32 674.0
USSR	9 925.0	14 470.0	22 806.0	30 256.0	34 634.0	36 675.0	38 227.0

· Amount unknown.
[1] Financial year ending on 30 June of year indicated. [2] Financial year ending on 31 March of year indicated. [3] Financial year ending on 31 March of year indicated (up to 1976). [4] Financial year ending on 31 March of year indicated (up to 1974). [5] Amount in 1961.

personnel, public assistance, benefits to war victims and public health services have been excluded.[2] The study thus covers the most substantial part of national social security systems.

The study covers a total of 31 countries, mostly industrialised, grouped as follows: 24 OECD countries and seven European countries with centrally planned economies. For nine EEC countries the study extends to 1980.

EVOLUTION OF SOCIAL SECURITY RECEIPTS IN RELATION TO GROWTH OF PRODUCT

Table 1 gives the basic data for the subsequent analyses. The table shows the total amount of social security receipts in millions of national monetary units (1960-77). These figures in themselves do not provide an indication of the real growth of receipts, owing to the effect of monetary depreciation; nor do they constitute a homogeneous basis for international comparison, as they are expressed in different monetary units.

Two series of indices have therefore been constructed. The first is the series of the indices of the evolution, by country, of social security receipts at constant (1975) prices. The second is the series of the indices of the evolution, by country, of the GDP or NMP during the same period (1960-77) at constant (1975) prices (see table 2).

Figure 1. Evolution of social security receipts as a percentage of GDP or NMP

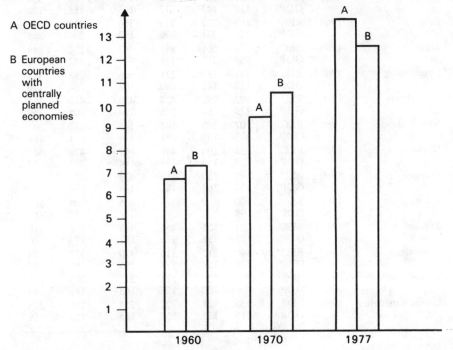

A OECD countries

B European countries with centrally planned economies

Financing social security: The options

Table 2. Indices of growth of social security receipts and of GDP or NMP at constant 1975 prices in OECD countries and European centrally planned economies, 1960-77

Country	Base year	Item	1965	1970	1974	1975	1976	1977
OECD countries								
Australia	1960	REC	138	178	255	302	399	451
		GDP	129	177	231	228	227	222
Austria	1960	REC	153	207	265	275	298	320
		GDP	123	159	196	193	205	213
Belgium	1960	REC	158	216	304	350	372	390
		GDP	128	162	197	194	204	206
Canada	1960	REC	132	335	509	569	592	601
		GDP	137	180	225	233	235	249
Denmark	1960	REC	157	237	329	371	403	443
		GDP	133	166	194	192	192	209
Finland	1960	REC	190	275	394	463	521	568
		GDP	129	174	210	212	212	213
France	1960	REC	158	.	358	394	427	460
		GDP	132	172	209	209	220	226
Germany (Fed. Rep. of)	1960	REC	137	183	246	279	296	299
		GDP	127	158	178	175	184	189
Greece	1965	REC	100	167	184	209	242	273
		GDP	100	142	171	181	193	200
Iceland	1960	REC	143	200	300	473	467	444
		GDP	138	154	208	207	214	227
Ireland	1960	REC	131	185	261	344	355	358
		GDP	119	149	177	183	188	198
Italy	1960	REC	164	232	335	310	328	354
		GDP	128	171	200	193	204	208
Japan	1960	REC	226	501	853	987	1 132	1 284
		GDP	184	311	438	436	442	472
Luxembourg	1960	REC	138	167	221	266	288	314
		GDP	118	142	180	163	168	170
Netherlands	1960	REC	173	296	429	456	489	494
		GDP	129	166	196	194	205	210
New Zealand	1960	REC	102	105	144	145	157	241
		GDP	129	139	182	174	171	181
Norway	1960	REC	155	296	445	462	478	471
		GDP	129	155	186	194	205	214
Portugal	1960	REC	173	250	312	437	451	.
		GDP	138	164	180	174	178	.
Spain	1960	REC	100	.	.	465	504	565
		GDP	98	.	.	173	178	183
Sweden	1960	REC	202	325	451	443	489	510
		GDP	129	156	171	172	174	170
Switzerland	1960	REC	140	212	316	320	337	349
		GDP	129	159	178	165	163	167
Turkey	1970	REC	.	100	172	216	269	301
		GDP	.	100	156	163	181	184
United Kingdom	1960	REC	130	178	222	254	255	275
		GDP	119	135	157	155	153	159

Table 2. *(concluded)*

Country	Base year	Item	1965	1970	1974	1975	1976	1977
United States	1960	REC	137	237	319	326	334	373
		GDP	125	146	165	164	173	182

European countries with centrally planned economies

Bulgaria	1961	REC	143	296	433	456	471	500
		NMP	132	203	271	294	315	332
Czechoslovakia	1970	REC	.	100	125	127	137	140
		NMP	.	100	122	130	135	140
German Demo-cratic Republic	1967	REC	.	121	177	183	191	211
		NMP	.	118	145	149	158	166
Hungary	1960	REC	136	210	317	359	387	405
		NMP	113	155	200	213	219	238
Romania	1960	REC	160	295	446	471	536	599
		NMP	154	227	350	385	427	465
USSR	1960	REC	145	229	305	349	369	384
		NMP	137	200	253	263	276	289

. Figure unknown.

REC = Social security receipts. GDP = Gross domestic product. NMP = Net material product.

Next, social security receipts have been expressed as a percentage of the GDP or NMP, and series constructed showing the evolution of these percentages, in each country and for all the countries covered taken together (table 3) (figure 1).

It will at once be noted that the percentage of GDP or NMP allocated to the financing of social security varies substantially from year to year but is in general growing systematically.

Secondly, comparison of the indices of social security receipts with those of GDP or NMP shows that the former grew more rapidly than the latter during the period 1960-77.

For a group of 23 countries (20 OECD countries and three centrally planned economies) for which complete data are available for the whole period 1960-77, the index value of social security receipts for 1977 (base year 1960 = 100) was 408, while the index value of GDP or NMP for 1977 was only 229.

This phenomenon can also be noted in the average annual rates of increase of index-series (table 4). The average annual rate of increase of social security receipts (23 countries) was 8.90 per cent in 1974 and 8.90 per cent again in 1977, whereas the average annual rate of increase of GDP or NMP was 5.33 per cent in 1974 and 4.77 per cent in 1977. These figures show that the allocation of resources to social security has not followed the slackening trend of economic growth in recent years.

An alternative approach is to compare the GDP or NMP per head of population with the percentage of GDP or NMP represented by social security receipts. Table 5 gives, for each group of countries, and for the

Table 3. Evolution of social security receipts as a percentage of GDP or NMP in OECD countries and European centrally planned economies, 1960-77 [1]

Country	1960	1965	1970	1974	1975	1976	1977
OECD countries							
Australia	5.21	5.55	5.25	5.75	6.88	9.15	10.56
Austria	10.75	13.34	13.93	14.52	15.33	15.62	16.19
Belgium	10.61	13.09	14.13	16.34	19.19	19.37	20.08
Canada	4.69	4.53	8.73	10.62	11.46	11.80	11.33
Denmark	6.33	7.48	9.03	10.72	12.19	13.30	13.43
Finland	4.81	7.07	7.59	9.02	10.53	11.82	12.83
France	9.24	11.03		15.85	17.40	17.99	18.83
Germany (Fed. Rep. of)	11.25	12.12	13.02	15.51	17.91	18.07	17.75
Greece		7.50	8.84	8.07	8.63	9.42	10.27
Iceland	6.24	6.49	8.08	9.00	14.28	13.62	12.24
Ireland	5.38	5.91	6.69	7.94	10.14	10.16	9.73
Italy	9.81	12.55	13.27	16.44	15.74	15.77	16.72
Japan	3.21	3.94	5.18	6.25	7.26	8.21	8.74
Luxembourg	11.81	13.76	13.92	14.51	19.25	20.30	21.78
Netherlands	9.91	13.32	17.60	21.63	23.25	23.66	23.25
New Zealand	9.17	7.22	6.92	7.25	7.64	8.39	12.21
Norway	6.52	7.86	12.49	15.60	15.55	15.20	14.38
Portugal	4.08	5.12	6.22	7.07	10.22	10.34	
Spain	3.76	3.86			10.12	10.64	11.63
Sweden	6.77	10.58	14.10	17.86	17.40	18.96	20.35
Switzerland	5.86	6.35	7.84	10.41	11.37	12.14	12.26
Turkey	1.20	1.58	2.47	2.72	3.28	3.67	4.04
United Kingdom	4.83	5.27	6.37	6.81	7.92	8.04	8.36
United States	3.44	3.77	5.58	6.63	6.85	6.62	7.02
European countries with centrally planned economies [2]							
Bulgaria	7.68 [3]	8.22	11.10	13.12	12.69	12.41	12.94
Czechoslovakia			13.17	13.35	13.02	13.87	14.42
German Democratic Republic		2.80 [4]	13.15	15.53	15.33	15.40	16.16
Hungary	8.75 [3]	10.65	10.95	13.56	14.84	15.31	15.13
Poland	6.01				8.08	8.66	9.27
Romania	5.57	5.90	7.30	7.27	7.01	7.21	7.46
USSR	6.84	7.48	7.87	8.55	9.53	9.51	9.42

. Figure unknown.

[1] For financial years ending on 31 March of year indicated (see table 1), the percentage relates to GDP of the preceding year. [2] For European countries with centrally planned economies, the percentage relates to NMP (Net material product) instead of GDP. [3] Year 1961. [4] Year 1967.

Table 4. Average annual rates of growth as a percentage of social security receipts and of GDP or NMP at constant 1975 prices in OECD countries and European centrally planned economies, 1960-77 (evolution since the first year of observation)

Country	First year of observation		1965	1970	1974	1975	1976	1977
OECD countries								
Australia	1960	REC	6.63	5.95	6.91	7.64	9.03	9.26
		GDP	5.30	5.89	6.17	5.66	5.26	4.82
Austria	1960	REC	8.86	7.53	7.20	6.99	7.06	7.09
		GDP	4.26	4.78	4.92	4.48	4.59	4.54
Belgium	1960	REC	9.59	8.00	8.25	8.71	8.56	8.34
		GDP	5.08	4.95	4.96	4.50	4.55	4.35
Canada	1960	REC	5.75	12.84	12.32	12.28	11.75	11.12
		GDP	6.52	6.05	5.96	5.80	5.50	5.51
Denmark	1960	REC	9.39	9.03	8.87	9.13	9.10	9.15
		GDP	5.80	5.22	4.85	4.46	4.15	4.42
Finland	1960	REC	13.69	10.63	10.29	10.76	10.87	10.76
		GDP	5.29	5.70	5.46	5.13	4.82	4.55
France	1960	REC	9.58	.	9.55	9.57	9.50	9.39
		GDP	5.77	5.58	5.40	5.04	5.04	4.90
Germany (Fed. Rep. of)	1960	REC	6.49	6.23	6.64	7.07	7.01	6.65
		GDP	4.92	4.69	4.22	3.81	3.89	3.82
Greece	1965	REC	.	10.81	7.01	7.64	8.38	8.74
		GDP	.	7.22	6.14	6.13	6.15	5.92
Iceland	1960	REC	7.41	7.17	8.15	10.92	10.11	9.17
		GDP	6.58	4.43	5.36	4.96	4.87	4.93
Ireland	1960	REC	5.48	6.36	7.10	8.59	8.23	7.80
		GDP	3.60	4.05	4.15	4.09	4.02	4.10
Italy	1960	REC	10.40	8.76	9.03	7.83	7.71	7.72
		GDP	5.10	5.52	5.08	4.48	4.56	4.39
Japan	1960	REC	17.74	17.49	16.55	16.49	16.37	16.20
		GDP	12.99	12.00	11.13	10.32	9.74	9.55
Luxembourg	1960	REC	6.64	5.26	5.82	6.73	6.84	6.97
		GDP	3.44	3.54	4.28	3.31	3.28	3.19
Netherlands	1960	REC	11.61	11.45	10.96	10.65	10.42	9.85
		GDP	5.19	5.22	4.94	4.53	4.58	4.47
New Zealand	1960	REC	0.32	0.46	2.64	2.51	2.85	5.30
		GDP	5.23	3.33	4.38	3.76	3.43	3.54
Norway	1960	REC	9.14	11.45	11.26	10.74	10.27	9.54
		GDP	5.16	4.45	4.54	4.51	4.59	4.57
Portugal	1960	REC	11.58	9.61	8.47	10.32	9.87	.
		GDP	6.63	5.08	4.29	3.77	3.66	.
Spain	1960	REC	0.05	.	.	10.79	10.63	10.73
		GDP	−0.48	.	.	3.71	3.66	3.60
Sweden	1960	REC	15.12	12.52	11.36	10.43	10.42	10.06
		GDP	5.28	4.57	3.91	3.69	3.54	3.16
Switzerland	1960	REC	6.92	7.82	8.57	8.07	7.90	7.62
		GDP	5.21	4.72	4.21	3.40	3.09	3.05
Turkey	1970	REC	.	.	14.55	16.66	17.94	17.04
		GDP	.	.	11.77	10.24	10.41	9.08

Table 4   *(concluded)*

Country	First year of observation		1965	1970	1974	1975	1976	1977
United Kingdom	1960	REC	5.41	5.93	5.85	6.41	6.03	6.14
		GDP	3.59	3.03	3.29	2.95	2.71	2.76
United States	1960	REC	6.58	9.01	8.64	8.21	7.82	8.06
		GDP	4.64	3.86	3.66	3.35	3.49	3.58
European countries with centrally planned economies[1]								
Bulgaria	1961	REC	9.38	12.83	11.93	11.44	10.88	10.58
		GDP	7.19	8.18	7.97	8.01	7.95	7.79
Czechoslovakia	1970	REC	.	3.94[2]	5.77	4.96	5.43	4.93
		GDP	.	4.90[2]	5.10	5.39	5.13	4.92
German Democratic Republic	1967	REC	.	6.55	8.52	7.88	7.45	7.76
		GDP	.	5.67	5.45	5.11	5.21	5.20
Hungary	1960	REC	8.04	8.61	9.28	9.55	9.44	9.14
		GDP	3.10	4.99	5.48	5.55	5.36	5.57
Romania	1960	REC	9.79	11.43	11.27	10.88	11.06	11.11
		GDP	9.02	8.54	9.36	9.40	9.50	9.46
USSR	1960	REC	7.68	8.63	8.29	8.68	8.51	8.23
		GDP	6.50	7.18	6.85	6.66	6.55	6.44

. Figure unknown.

REC = Social security receipts. GDP = Gross domestic product. NMP = Net material product.

[1] For European countries with centrally planned economies, the percentages relate to NMP (Net material product) instead of GDP.   [2] Year 1971.

years 1960, 1970 and 1977, the GDP or NMP per head of population in US dollars, the percentage of GDP or NMP represented by social security receipts, and also the average annual rate of increase of the total product and total receipts (at constant 1975 prices). The table leads to the same conclusion: the rate of growth of social security receipts significantly exceeds that of GDP or NMP.

EVOLUTION OF THE DISTRIBUTION OF RECEIPTS BY SOURCE

Table 6 gives the distribution (in percentage) of social security receipts by source at the beginning of the period of observation (generally 1960) and in 1977. Table 7 and figure 2 show, for the two groups of countries, the average percentages of the different sources of financing.

This table shows that on the whole there were no substantial changes in the distribution of social security receipts by source over the period considered. As far as the OECD countries are concerned, a slight shift in the distribution from the insured persons towards the employers is apparent, as also a small decrease in the relative share of public authorities. In the European countries with centrally planned economies, there was a moderate shift of contributions from insured persons and employers to the public authorities.

Table 5. Evolution of GDP or NMP per head of population and of social security receipts as a percentage of the national product in OECD countries and European centrally planned economies, 1960-77

Years and items	OECD countries	Countries with centrally planned economies
1960		
GDP or NMP per head of population (US$)	1 185	604
Social security receipts as a percentage of GDP or NMP	6.73	7.21
1970		
GDP or NMP per head of population (US$)	2 444	1 133
Social security receipts as a percentage of GDP or NMP	9.42	10.59
1977		
GDP or NMP per head of population (US$)	6 401	2 423
Social security receipts as a percentage of GDP or NMP	13.52	12.58
Average annual percentage rate of increase–		
of total GDP or NMP	4.60	6.56
of total social security receipts	9.27	8.63

In the centrally planned economies the employer and state contributions are much larger than in the other countries and interest on capital is non-existent.

It must be realised, however, that these averages concerning the various sources of financing hide very divergent trends in a number of countries.

In fact, table 6 indicates that in some cases there have been significant changes in the method of social security financing. For example, the contributions of insured persons have been substantially reduced in Denmark, Iceland, Norway and Sweden. This reduction has been offset by a significant increase, in Denmark in the contributions of the public authorities, and in Iceland, Norway and Sweden in the employers' contribution and in income from capital; in the last two countries there was also a substantial fall in the contribution of the public authorities.

EVOLUTION OF RECEIPTS IN NINE EEC COUNTRIES FROM 1977 TO 1980

Although the international analysis cannot be carried beyond 1977, the terminal year of the ILO's last inquiry into the cost of social security, it is possible to pursue the study for nine EEC countries up to 1980, although on a substantially different basis, using data from other sources. This supplementary study is not without methodological difficulties, but it throws some light at least on the question whether the trends detected up to 1977 have or have not been maintained during these last years.

Financing social security: The options

Table 6. Distribution of social security receipts by origin as a percentage of total receipts in OECD countries and European centrally planned economies, 1960 and 1977

Country	Year	Insured persons	Employers	Public authorities	Income from capital	Other receipts
OECD countries						
Australia	1959-60	7.6	11.1	80.4	0.8	0.1
	1976-77	12.3	10.0	77.2	0.4	0.1
Austria	1960	32.3	50.3	14.4	0.9	2.1
	1977	32.4	42.5	21.8	0.6	2.7
Belgium	1960	23.4	42.2	27.1	3.7	3.6
	1977	20.8	43.1	32.7	2.7	0.7
Canada	1959-60	9.0	16.3	70.5	4.0	0.2
	1976-77	9.1	15.0	70.9	4.9	0.1
Denmark	1959-60	24.2	5.1	69.8	0.9	.
	1977	2.6	3.4	90.9	3.1	.
Finland	1960	17.5	50.1	19.3	13.0	0.1
	1977	17.5	63.8	10.9	7.8	.
France	1960	18.9	68.9	11.1	0.3	0.8
	1977	23.9	65.4	8.7	1.2	0.8
Germany (Fed. Rep. of)	1960	37.4	40.8	17.7	3.3	0.8
	1977	38.3	39.6	19.8	1.6	0.7
Greece	1965	38.2	35.6	20.4	5.0	0.8
	1977	35.3	38.6	19.4	4.7	2.0
Iceland	1960	20.0	11.0	64.2	4.8	.
	1977	5.6	17.4	62.8	11.0	3.2
Ireland	1959-60	8.6	15.7	73.9	1.8	.
	1977	16.4	30.3	52.8	0.4	0.1
Italy	1960	12.6	64.6	18.2	2.2	2.4
	1977	15.8	65.3	14.4	3.0	1.5
Japan	1959-60	36.3	40.6	13.6	6.0	3.5
	1976-77	30.6	30.1	22.2	8.7	8.4
Luxembourg	1960	26.9	42.0	20.7	9.5	0.9
	1977	29.0	35.6	22.1	7.7	5.6
Netherlands	1960	49.4	38.9	5.9	5.8	.
	1977	44.1	36.3	14.6	4.5	0.5
New Zealand	1959-60	.	4.5	95.4	.	0.1
	1976-77	.	4.2	95.8	.	.
Norway	1959-60	39.8	26.7	31.2	2.0	0.3
	1977	29.7	52.3	17.6	0.4	.
Portugal	1960	19.2	59.9	0.8	14.0	6.1
	1976	21.2	73.0	3.2	1.9	0.7
Spain	1960	21.7	68.6	3.4	5.3	1.0
	1977	17.5	76.3	4.0	1.0	1.2
Sweden	1960	33.6	9.1	54.7	2.6	.
	1977	2.0	65.1	20.5	12.4	.
Switzerland	1960	48.5	25.9	13.5	10.9	1.2
	1977	48.2	24.5	21.8	4.8	0.7
Turkey	1960	36.4	56.0	.	6.1	1.5
	1977	37.4	47.4	.	12.8	2.4
United Kingdom	1959-60	34.2	34.4	28.6	2.2	0.6
	1976-77	30.7	47.1	19.3	2.8	0.1

Table 6   *(concluded)*

Country	Year	Insured persons	Employers	Public authorities	Income from capital	Other receipts
United States	1959-60	36.7	58.3	.	5.0	.
	1976-77	38.8	52.0	6.2	3.0	.

European countries with centrally planned economies

Bulgaria	1961	0.9	85.7	8.0	.	5.4
	1977	.	69.9	22.2	.	7.9
Czechoslovakia	1970	0.1	3.8	96.1	.	.
	1977	.	3.5	96.5	.	.
German Democratic Republic	1967	32.9	35.6	31.3	.	0.2
	1977	23.5	26.0	50.4	.	0.1
Hungary	1961	13.1	49.2	37.2	0.1	0.4
	1977	16.2	46.7	36.5	.	0.6
Romania	1960	.	67.4	32.6	.	.
	1977	.	76.3	23.7	.	.
USSR	1965	.	.	95.6	.	4.4
	1977	.	.	.	.	.

. Figure unknown.

The countries chosen are the nine members of the EEC before the accession of Greece, and the data used are drawn from the social accounts of the Statistical Office of the European Communities. These data concern social protection in the sense given to the term by the EEC, namely, the financing of pensions and services for sickness, invalidity, handicap, employment injuries, old age, survivors, maternity, family, placement, vocational guidance, occupational mobility, unemployment and housing benefits. The field covered is therefore considerably broader than that of the ILO inquiry.[3]

Three tables have been compiled for the period 1977-80: one on the evolution of social protection receipts as a percentage of GDP (table 8), another on trends in the distribution of receipts by source (table 9) and the third on the evolution of indices of receipts and GDP at constant 1975 prices (table 10). Since the series of studies for 1960-77 and this complementary study are not homogeneous, tables 8 and 9 repeat for the year 1977 the results previously indicated for the social insurance and allied systems as well as the results of the ILO inquiry for social security schemes in the broad sense (including schemes covering civil servants and military personnel, public assistance, benefits to war victims and public health).[4] These last figures are much closer to those obtained from the EEC social protection accounts.

Financing social security: The options

Table 7. Average percentages of different sources of social security financing in OECD countries and European centrally planned economies, 1960 and 1977

Country group	Year	Insured persons	Employers	Public authorities	Income from capital	Other receipts	Total
OECD countries (24)	1960	26.4	36.5	31.4	4.6	1.1	100
	1977	23.3	40.8	30.4	4.2	1.3	100
	Difference	−3.1	+4.3	−1.0	−0.4	+0.2	0
Countries with centrally planned economies (5)	1960	9.4	48.3	41.1	–	1.2	100
	1977	7.9	44.5	45.9	–	1.7	100
	Difference	−1.5	−3.8	+4.8	–	+0.5	0

Figure 2. Average percentages of different sources of social security financing

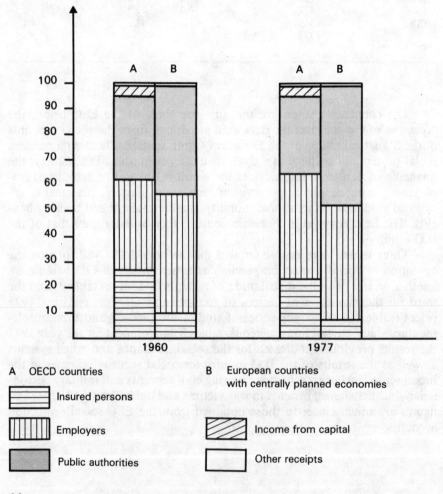

A   OECD countries

B   European countries with centrally planned economies

- Insured persons
- Employers
- Public authorities
- Income from capital
- Other receipts

Table 8. Receipts of social insurance (SI), social security (SS) and social protection (SP) as a percentage of GDP in nine EEC countries, 1977-80

Country	Scheme	1977	1978	1979	1980
Belgium	SI	20.08	.	.	.
	SS	25.59	.	.	.
	SP	26.70	26.48	26.75	27.29
Denmark	SI	13.43	.	.	.
	SS	24.55	.	.	.
	SP	26.54	27.81	28.61	29.44
France	SI	18.83	.	.	.
	SS	25.99	.	.	.
	SP	24.93	25.30	26.21	26.93
Germany	SI	17.75	.	.	.
(Fed. Rep. of)	SS	23.00	.	.	.
	SP	29.51	29.60	28.98	29.37
Ireland	SI	9.73	.	.	.
	SS	18.37	.	.	.
	SP	18.45	17.59	19.40	22.23
Italy	SI	16.72	.	.	.
	SS	20.83	.	.	.
	SP	21.83	24.82	25.30	24.11
Luxembourg	SI	21.78	.	.	.
	SS	27.10	.	.	.
	SP	28.91	27.60	27.04	28.46
Netherlands	SI	23.25	.	.	.
	SS	31.44	.	.	.
	SP	35.50	34.92	36.19	37.21
United Kingdom	SI	8.36	.	.	.
	SS	18.78	.	.	.
	SP	24.07	23.92	24.16	25.27
EEC (average)	SI	16.66	.	.	.
	SS	23.96	.	.	.
	SP	26.27	26.45	26.96	27.81

. Figure unknown.

Table 8 shows that the average receipts for social protection as a percentage of GDP in the nine countries continued to grow up to 1980: 26.27 per cent in 1977 and 27.81 in 1980. This average, however, evens out very varied trends in the different countries. Whereas the upward trend was marked in Ireland, Denmark and Italy, there was a slight downturn in the Federal Republic of Germany and Luxembourg. Table 10, in which the indices of receipts and GDP are compared, also brings out the disparities between the countries and shows that the rising percentage in Denmark was above all due to the drop in GDP (the rise in the index of receipts was much less there than in most of the other countries).

As regards the source of receipts, for the average of the countries there is a shift in the employers' share towards the public authorities that was not observed in the preceding period. Insured persons' contributions also show a very slight increase.

Table 9. Trends in the percentage distribution of receipts of social insurance (SI), social security (SS) and social protection (SP) by source in nine EEC countries, 1977-80

Country (and currency)	Scheme	Year	Employers	Insured persons	Current public contributions	Other receipts	Total (millions of national currency units)
Belgium (Belgian franc)	SI	1977	43.1	20.8	32.7	3.4	570 025.5
	SS	1977	41.7	18.1	35.3	4.9	726 236.5
	SP	1977	41.7	18.6	33.8	5.9	742 040
		1978	40.9	20.4	34.1	4.6	790 790
		1979	40.7	20.2	34.5	4.6	852 020
		1980	41.0	20.1	34.7	4.2	929 630
Denmark (Danish kroner)	SI	1977	3.4	2.6	90.9	3.1	37 375.6
	SS	1977	5.5	1.4	91.4	1.7	68 320.6
	SP	1977	11.3	1.8	83.3	3.6	75 191
		1978	10.6	1.9	83.5	4.0	86 648
		1979	10.4	2.1	83.9	3.6	98 966
		1980	9.7	1.8	85.0	3.5	110 129
France (French franc)	SI	1977	65.4	23.9	8.7	2.0	353 172.1
	SS	1977	55.7	19.4	23.2	1.7	487 352.4
	SP	1977	57.9	21.0	17.7	3.4	468 770
		1978	57.7	20.7	18.5	3.1	541 500
		1979	56.2	22.4	18.4	3.0	639 400
		1980	56.0	23.7	17.6	2.7	741 790
Germany (Fed. Rep. of) (DM)	SI	1977	39.6	38.3	19.8	2.3	212 528
	SS	1977	41.1	29.5	26.4	3.0	275 312
	SP	1977	41.8	28.4	25.6	4.2	354 300
		1978	42.6	27.7	25.6	4.1	380 760
		1979	43.4	27.3	25.6	3.7	403 910
		1980	42.7	27.5	26.7	3.1	437 300
Ireland (Irish pound)	SI	1977	30.3	16.4	52.8	0.5	523.40
	SS	1977	25.3	11.4	60.8	2.5	938.28
	SP	1977	25.6	11.4	60.5	2.5	996.20
		1978	26.1	12.8	60.3	0.8	1 138.20

	Series	Year					
Italy (Italian lira)	SI	1977	65.3	15.8	14.4	4.5	28 921 000
	SS	1977	61.2	13.5	21.2	4.1	36 034 000
	SP	1978	68.3	10.4	17.7	3.6	41 501 000
		1979	60.1	9.4	27.1	3.4	55 171 000
		1980	57.8	12.6	26.6	3.0	68 234 000
			58.8	13.6	24.9	2.7	81 354 000
Luxembourg (Luxembourg franc)	SI	1977	35.6	29.0	22.1	13.3	22 038.1
	SS	1977	38.8	25.6	24.8	10.8	27 424.2
	SP	1978	36.9	24.6	30.9	7.6	29 023
		1979	36.0	24.2	31.5	8.3	30 887
		1980	35.5	23.2	31.7	9.6	33 650
			36.1	22.9	31.6	9.4	38 073
Netherlands (guilder)	SI	1977	36.3	44.1	14.6	5.0	61 022.8
	SS	1977	38.2	35.7	18.0	8.1	82 502.7
	SP	1978	39.2	32.5	18.4	9.9	92 793
		1979	37.8	32.1	19.9	10.2	103 712
		1980	37.7	31.7	19.9	10.7	113 919
			37.1	31.0	20.4	11.5	124 016
United Kingdom (pound sterling)	SI	1976-77[1]	47.1	30.7	19.3	2.9	10 288
	SS	1976-77[1]	29.5	17.7	50.5	2.3	23 120
	SP	1977	35.2	15.7	40.7	8.4	34 343
		1978	34.7	14.7	42.2	8.4	40 121
		1979	34.6	14.8	41.8	8.8	48 643
		1980	33.3	14.6	43.6	8.5	58 476
EEC (average)	SI	1977	40.7	24.6	30.6	4.1	
	SS	1977	37.5	19.1	39.1	4.3	
	SP	1978	39.8	18.2	36.5	5.5	
		1979	38.5	18.2	38.1	5.2	
		1980	38.0	18.5	38.2	5.3	
			37.8	18.5	38.5	5.2	

[1] Financial year beginning on 1 April 1976 and ending on 31 March 1977.

47

Table 10.   Indices of social protection receipts and of GDP at constant 1975 prices in nine
EEC countries, 1977-80

Country	Year	GDP	Social protection receipts
Belgium	1977	100	100
	1978	101.6	100.7
	1979	103.6	103.8
Denmark	1977	100	100
	1978	98.2	102.9
	1979	99.4	107.2
	1980	95.8	106.3
France	1977	100	100
	1978	104.4	105.9
	1979	107.4	112.9
	1980	106.8	115.3
Germany (Fed. Rep. of)	1977	100	100
	1978	103.5	103.8
	1979	107.8	105.8
	1980	109.1	108.6
Ireland	1977	100	100
	1978	112.3	107.1
	1979	114.1	119.9
	1980	112.5	135.5
Italy	1977	100	100
	1978	107.2	121.9
	1979	113.4	131.4
	1980	117.0	129.2
Luxembourg	1977	100	100
	1978	105.6	100.9
	1979	112.4	105.1
	1980	113.7	111.9
Netherlands	1977	100	100
	1978	108.8	107.1
	1979	110.6	112.7
	1980	109.5	114.7
United Kingdom	1977	100	100
	1978	104.8	104.1
	1979	110.9	111.3
	1980	108.0	113.4

Notes

[1] ILO: *The cost of social security*, op. cit.

[2] The whole of the receipts included in table 7 of the ILO publication *The cost of social security*, op. cit.

[3] ibid., p. 16, and EUROSTAT.

[4] The receipts included in tables 1, 2, 3 and 4 of the ILO publication *The cost of social security*, op. cit.

PART TWO

FINANCING PROBLEMS AND NATIONAL EXPERIENCE

SOCIAL SECURITY FINANCING METHODS, LABOUR COSTS AND EMPLOYMENT IN INDUSTRIALISED MARKET ECONOMY COUNTRIES

3

Alain and Chantal Euzéby *

INTRODUCTION

Among the multiple and often contradictory ideas, reflections and criticisms to which social security financing methods have given rise, the question of their impact on labour costs and employment is one which is being increasingly articulated. This can be explained by the fact that after almost 30 years of exceptionally rapid and relatively balanced economic growth, most of the industrialised market economy countries have been confronted, since the watershed years of 1973-74, with the worst economic crisis they have experienced since 1929. The increase in the price of energy and raw materials, the collapse of the international monetary system based on fixed exchange rates and the intensification of international competition (in particular from newly industrialised countries where labour is cheap) have in most cases led to a very marked slowdown in economic growth and the co-existence of high levels of inflation and unemployment.

Faced with this new situation, most of the industrialised market economy countries have opted for industrial redeployment and the reinforcement of international specialisation (the new international division of labour). Under such an option, the balance of payments situation constitutes the main obstacle to national development. Industrial competitivity thus becomes one of the principal objectives of economic policy, with the holding down of labour costs (wages plus social charges) constituting an instrument of economic policy.

It is in this general context that the question of the relationship between social security financing methods, labour costs and employment must be placed. The financial problems raised for social security by the ageing of the population, the often spiralling costs of medical care, the spread of unemployment or the new requirements of social legislation only make the question more acute. The combination of these financial prob-

---

* Lecturers, Faculty of Economic Science, University of Grenoble (France).

51

lems with the economic difficulties due to the crisis is undoubtedly responsible for the recent proliferation of proposals and measures put forward as remedies for the real or alleged defects of current financing methods.

Social security at the level it has reached in industrialised countries today calls for the expenditure of vast sums, representing from 20 to 30 per cent of GDP in the countries where it is most developed. The main sources of these funds are payroll contributions based chiefly on employment earnings, particularly wages, and tax receipts, although in widely differing proportions according to whether the system draws more heavily on the laws of Bismarck or the ideas of Beveridge.

When social benefits are financed from general taxation, the problem of financing does not arise in any specific way. It is in fact part of a more general question concerning the overall structure of the taxation system understood in the strict sense of the term.[1] It is essentially contributions and in particular employers' contributions which, since they are levied only on wages, are often blamed for increasing labour costs and, by extension, for slowing down employment.

It will be noted that the social security system of charges and benefits does on the whole have a positive influence on employment since beneficiaries generally have a high propensity to consume. The redistribution of income which is achieved by social security between the healthy and the sick, the economically active and the retired, persons with a job and those who are unemployed, single persons or married couples without children and persons who have family responsibilities (horizontal redistribution) and, as the case may be, between the rich and the poor (vertical redistribution) as a result of the methods used for calculating charges and benefits, does in effect tend to increase the nation's average propensity to consume and stimulate global demand and employment. Viewed from this perspective, benefits produce an anti-cyclical effect which is particularly useful in periods of economic recession and high unemployment.

But the methods used to finance benefits are neither neutral nor equivalent. Their economic and social implications vary, are open to contradictory interpretation, and are closely related to the defence of the individual interests of the various socio-occupational groups concerned. Thus, any reform project will inevitably give rise to animosity, since at the level of the impact on real disposable income, it is impossible to improve the situation of one group without adversely affecting that of others.

It is therefore not sufficient to examine in what way the system of payroll contributions, and in particular employers' contributions, may slow down the use of manpower; it must also be asked whether other financing methods could, with an identical volume of resources, exert a more favourable influence on employment. The problems involved and the possible solutions will therefore be considered in turn.

THE PROBLEMS INVOLVED

There is every likelihood that the coming years will continue to be characterised by the rising cost of energy and raw materials, growing competition from the newly industrialised countries with cheap labour and the intensification of competition between industrialised countries. None of the latter can thus afford to allow its currency to depreciate on the exchange market without running the risk of seeing its terms of trade deteriorate and being obliged to pay even more for indispensable energy and raw materials.

The policy the industrialised market economy countries have chosen is that of greater integration within the world economy. More precisely, the major objective is to ensure some approach to balanced foreign trade by enabling industry not only to withstand certain imports, but also to export more and more so as to finance the increasing cost of imported energy and raw materials. Success in meeting this challenge depends on the competitivity of firms. It implies reinforcement of the international division of labour, gradual renunciation of the least competitive sectors and reconversion of industrial activities towards high technology sectors.

The basic idea is as follows: if developing countries are able, by means of their cheap labour, to compete with the industrialised countries in those sectors which require a large supply of unskilled labour, the industrialised countries must react by concentrating on peak research-orientated activities demanding a highly skilled workforce. This assumes a permanent effort on the part of enterprises in the industrialised countries to modernise, innovate and adapt their production to foreign demands.

It is in the context of this basic option of industrial redeployment that the relationship between social security financing methods, labour costs and employment should be examined. In the hope of shedding some light on an area where gratuitous affirmations and counter-affirmations are legion, in the following pages an attempt will be made to evaluate the importance and implications of the various problems involved by examining them under the four following heads: labour costs and employment; social security financing and labour costs; the exclusive use of wages as the contribution base; the application of a ceiling to the contribution base.

Labour costs and employment

This question will be examined first from the negative standpoint of the ways in which high labour costs can fuel unemployment and secondly, from the positive viewpoint of why curtailing such costs is likely to increase industrial competitivity.

Labour costs and unemployment

High labour costs can never be more than one of many possible causes of unemployment. The widespread nature of unemployment can in fact be explained by factors–which vary from country to country–such as: the appearance on the labour market of persons born during high birth-rate periods at a time when the persons reaching retirement age correspond to low birth-rate periods; a very marked increase in the number of economically active women; a general slowdown in economic growth and production investment, related in particular to increases in energy costs and financial charges borne by enterprises or fluctuations in the money and financial markets, which make investment operations especially hazardous; slow restructuring of industries and insufficient modernisation of production in the sectors most vulnerable to keen foreign competition; the rural exodus uncompensated by the creation of enough jobs in industry and services; lack of synchronisation between the skills required for the jobs proposed on the one hand, and the qualifications and skills or aspirations of young persons on the other; an increase in unemployment benefit which apparently tends to prolong the time spent in the search for employment.[2]

However, high labour costs can have a specific impact on two kinds of unemployment which have developed jointly since the end of the 1960s: they can encourage the increase of classic unemployment and the continuation of Keynesian unemployment.

"Classic" unemployment may be defined as unemployment which is related to the fact that labour costs are too high in proportion to productivity and above the cost at which labour supply and demand would balance. This situation not only has a direct negative effect on recruitment, but also reduces profits and investment, which in turn discourages employment.[3]

High labour costs and inflexible resistance to their reduction tend to diminish firms' actual or potential profits, and consequently restrict their capacity or readiness to invest. This has negative repercussions on employment for two main reasons, first, because a small increase in productive capacity is insufficient to absorb available manpower, secondly, because the inadequacy of the profits earned by firms which are vulnerable to increasingly keen international competition is prejudicial to their modernisation and ability to produce at competitive prices, and hence to their exports and their capacity to withstand imports. Moreover, this phenomenon is an inducement to enterprises to decentralise part of their activities, particularly those requiring a large supply of labour, by setting up in countries where the levels of wages and social protection are low.

Keynesian unemployment is unemployment due to insufficient demand resulting from a general slowing down of economic growth. As a component of global demand, a decline in investment activity due to high labour costs serves to fuel this kind of unemployment.

Labour costs and industrial competitivity

Competitivity may be defined in general terms as the capacity to face foreign competition or more specifically, the capacity to obtain high profit margins without compromising the competitivity of selling prices: supremacy over foreign competitors in terms of cost price is thus the first condition for success.[4] For firms to be able to meet the challenge of foreign competition, it is in their interest to have the lowest possible production costs. Labour costs have a special place in production costs and are more often than not considered to be an important–if not the most important–component affecting competitivity.[5]

Staff costs are indeed the main component of the value added and a determining factor in the geographical siting of activities. Moreover, the gap between production costs in the industrialised countries and those of the Third World countries is essentially the expression of the difference in the average hourly wage; geographical variations in the prices of raw materials are less marked owing to the greater international mobility of these production factors.[6] Whilst there may be a world price for such-and-such a commodity or a standard interest rate, there can be no global wage rate. The cost of labour varies on average from 1 to 8 between the market economy industrialised countries and the newly industrialised countries of the Third World.

The cost of labour influences the selling price both directly, in as far as it is a component of the latter, and indirectly, to the extent that it conditions the self-financing capacity of an enterprise and by extension, its investment and modernisation possibilities. Thus any increase in labour costs is likely to result in higher wage costs per unit produced (hourly wage cost/hourly productivity of the work), which is a good productivity indicator. In effect it leads to an immediate increase in the hourly wage cost and to a subsequent slow down or decline in productivity as a result of lower profits and investment.

The impact of labour costs on the selling price and thus on competitivity is, however, also dependent on the evolution of the exchange rate. Generally speaking, a reduction in this cost factor will tend to stimulate exports, slow down imports and thereby, in a system of floating exchange rates, improve the exchange rate. This improvement leads to a reduction in the cost of imports and therefore tends to reduce inflation and have a moderating influence on wages.

Consequently, in an international economic context, in which employment depends to a large extent on industrial competitivity, control of labour costs serves more and more often as an instrument of labour policy: by reducing production costs per unit produced and increasing profits and investments, it acts as a stimulus to employment. It is therefore through their impact on labour costs that the size and methods of collecting social security funds are apt to affect the level of employment.

Social security financing and labour costs [7]

Contrary to what is sometimes asserted, the part represented by employers' contributions in the financing of social security, in the total cost of labour or in the sum of the compulsory charges does not explain the differences between labour costs in various countries. Where international comparisons are available they show in fact that these differences are much more closely related to the gap separating direct wages and global tax pressure (taxation plus social contributions) than to social security financing methods. Table 11 shows clearly that there is no correlation between total labour costs and the share of the social charges of an enterprise represented by these costs or by employers' contributions in compulsory charges taken as a whole. The table shows in particular that although the percentage of employers' contributions to the whole of compulsory charges is highest in France, Italy and Spain, these countries are far from having the highest labour costs. The case of Denmark, with its relatively high labour costs and particularly low employers' contributions is equally symptomatic.[8] The choice between relatively low wages, high social charges and relatively low taxation on the one hand, and high wages, low social charges and relatively high taxation on the other, has therefore hardly any impact on the total cost of labour.

This can be explained essentially in terms of the "tax-push inflation effect". Highlighted in several studies,[9] and common to all compulsory charges, this effect is the result of the impetus given to inflation by the increases in taxation or social contributions needed to finance greater public expenditure or social benefits. The parties affected consider the purchasing power of their available income after deduction of compulsory charges, without really taking into account the advantages they receive in terms of public expenditure and social benefits, with the result that any increase in taxation or contributions tends to have repercussions on the processes which determine prices and wages. These repercussions are closely related to the power of the trade unions and the mechanisms indexing wages on the general price level. Consequently, the financing of greater social security expenditure by means of obligations imposed directly on households rather than enterprises does not necessarily leave labour costs unaffected, unless it is accompanied by a mandatory or negotiated freezing of wages, or the suppression of their indexing on the cost of living. This corresponds to a political choice, which involves imposing social benefits on individuals to the detriment of income at their free disposal.

Although every increase in social security expenditure tends to have direct or indirect repercussions on labour costs, the repercussions are not necessarily uniform. They may vary in intensity according to the financing methods employed. Hence the interest, for economies which are vulnerable to increasingly fierce international constraints, in having recourse to the kind of charges least likely to affect labour costs. Thus, social security financing reform projects are more and more frequently being conceived as a means of lightening the burden on enterprises without prejudice to advantages already acquired, or as a way of meeting increased expenditure without imposing heavier charges on enterprises. It is in this context that the

Table 11.   Social security, compulsory charges and labour costs in industry in 16 OECD
countries, 1979

Country	Hourly wage costs (in DM)	Average hourly wage (in DM)	Social charges per hour (in DM)	Social charges as a percentage of wage costs	Employers' contributions as a percentage of total compulsory charges (1978)	Compulsory charges as a percentage of GDP (1978)
Austria	14.14	7.56	6.58	46.5	15.3	41.4
Belgium	21.53	12.41	9.12	42.3	19.3	44.2
Canada	15.05	11.71	3.34	22.2	.	31.1
Denmark	20.29	16.80	3.49	17.2	0.5	43.6
France	15.05	8.41	6.64	44.1	29.7	39.7
Germany (Fed. Rep. of)	21.14	12.46	8.68	41.0	18.2	37.8
Greece	6.25	4.11	2.14	34.2	14.4	22.5
Ireland	8.98	6.96	2.02	22.5	8.7	33.4
Italy	15.25	7.33	7.92	51.9	27.7	32.6
Japan	11.77	9.69	2.08	17.7	15.3	24.1
Netherlands	21.18	12.07	9.11	43.0	16.8	46.8
Spain	10.16	6.39	3.77	37.0	39.7	22.8
Sweden	21.36	12.95	8.41	39.4	25.6	53.5
Switzerland	20.62	14.22	6.40	31.0	10.3	31.5
United Kingdom	10.20	7.85	2.35	23.0	10.8	34.4
United States	16.95	12.24	4.71	27.8	14.9	30.2

. Figure unknown.

Sources: Institut der Deutschen Wirtschaft (IW): *IW–Trends 1980* (Cologne, 1980); OECD: *Revenue statistics of OECD member countries, 1965-79* (Paris, 1980).

various possible solutions presented in the second part of this chapter will be examined.

Contributions based exclusively on wages

The fact of basing social charges solely on income from employment means in effect that employers' contributions are found entirely at the expense of wages and consequently obtained from only one production factor: labour. Such contributions are therefore often criticised as being a real factor of unemployment, first, because they encourage the replacement of men by machines (capital/labour substitution), secondly, because they penalise labour-intensive enterprises. This is why it has often been suggested that employers' contributions should be imposed on a wider base, such as the total value added. The serious disadvantages of this kind of solution will be discussed in the second part of this chapter. The following paragraphs will be concerned with the question of the extent to which the use of the wage bill as the sole base for employers' contributions can really be considered one of the causes of unemployment.

The problem of capital/labour substitution

It is undeniable that enterprises will be inclined to favour production techniques which, given the relative costs of the factors of labour and capital, allow them to keep their production costs down to a minimum. But does this necessarily mean that employers' contributions based solely on wages exert a negative effect on employment by encouraging capital substitution at the expense of labour? Such a view appears to be exaggerated for two sets of reasons.

In the first place, the part played by employers' contributions in capital/labour substitution is often overestimated. What counts in this process is the relative cost of labour vis-à-vis capital. The global cost of labour (wages plus social charges) is, as was noted above, much more influenced by the volume of direct wages and the pressure from taxation in the widest sense of the term (total compulsory transfers as a percentage of GDP) than by the role played by employers' contributions in the total compulsory charges. The tax-push inflation effect shows that other transfers (direct or indirect taxation) also tend to influence labour costs.

On the other hand, the cost of capital is significantly reduced by various measures taken in many countries to encourage investment. Whether such measures take the form of subsidies, tax deductions, loans granted at preferential interest rates or incentives to long-term saving, they all serve to accelerate the accumulation of capital by making it easier to obtain financial resources and/or by reducing the cost of capital utilisation. Investment aid systems are today of special importance in the industrialised countries' arsenal of economic policy instruments. The array of tax measures is particularly comprehensive [10] and exerts a very marked influence on the cost of capital utilisation. [11]

Finally, it should be noted that employers' contributions are charges which determine a firm's cost and selling prices. There is thus every likelihood that an increase in the rate of these contributions will result in a general increase in prices and therefore indirectly but effectively push up capital equipment costs. Distortions between the cost of labour and the cost of capital due to an increase in employers' contributions are therefore in reality much less important than might be supposed if only their direct repercussions on labour costs are considered.

Furthermore, capital/labour substitution tends rather to encourage employment, which brings us to the second set of reasons.

In economies that are broadly open to international trade, it is above all technological progress and the pressure of international competition which encourage capital/labour substitution. The modernisation which results from firms' investment efforts enables them to reduce their cost and selling prices. It thus tends to stimulate exports, increase resistance to imports and thereby exert a positive influence on employment. What is of paramount importance to labour costs is, in reality, the global cost per unit produced. To the extent that investment leads to a reduction in this cost and better adaptation to domestic and international market conditions, it serves to promote employment.

The United Kingdom is a case in point. Although British labour costs are much lower than those of most other EEC countries, labour is much less productive there because of qualitative and quantitative deficiencies in the stock of capital.[12] This weakness in investment and innovation is one of the most obvious signs of the decline in production in the United Kingdom and has led to a marked increase in the rate at which foreign imports have penetrated the country (imports as a percentage of domestic demand).[13]

A distinction is generally made between two kinds of investment. The first, capacity investments, are those that create jobs by expanding productive capacity. They are characterised by an employment cost, a certain amount of investment expenditure per job created, which varies considerably from branch to branch. The second are productivity or modernisation investments, the purpose of which is to reduce expenditure on energy, raw materials or labour. In the last case, such investments encourage capital/labour substitution and sometimes provoke hostile reactions against "machines which are replacing workers". In reality, the relationship between productive investments and employment is ambivalent, for whilst such investments allow firms and sectors to economise on labour, they also constitute a component of global demand and have a positive impact on employment in the sectors that make them.

Furthermore, it may be asked why the productivity gains generated by these investments should necessarily result in the loss of jobs. In economies exposed to strong foreign competition, they may on the contrary stimulate employment by protecting firms' competitivity and enabling them to shoulder increased labour costs. Productivity gains are also a prerequisite for any reduction in hours of work without an accompanying reduction in wages.

It is therefore questionable whether a reduction in labour costs (in particular one due to lower employers' contributions) checks capital/labour substitution. It may indeed be an incentive to firms to use their extra financial resources to make productivity investments. In this case, lower labour costs tend to stimulate employment not so much because they reduce capital/labour substitution but because they enable firms to be more competitive.

The idea that the slowing down of technological progress and investment is favourable to employment is a dangerous one.[14] It is more appropriate to stress the *complementary nature* of investments and employment; any effort to increase exports or strengthen resistance to foreign imports by the modernisation of equipment and production processes automatically increases the rate of investment. It was in this sense that the CEE experts noted, in a document prepared for the 1978 Tripartite Conference, that investments designed to reduce labour costs are not in themselves negative:

Even when the primary concern is to maximise employment, it is important not to discourage investments which permit savings to be made in manpower. In the very short term, such investments are an element of demand and as such have a positive impact on employment. In the medium term, they play a vital role by protecting competitivity. In times of intense competition, a producer who does not make investments to reduce his costs will in the end have to close his doors. Orders and jobs will go elsewhere–to Japan, for example, This is why investments that reduce costs should be viewed in a favourable light as a means of establishing solid foundations for employment in the long term in vast sectors of the economy.

Furthermore, it is extremely important, in a study of investments designed to reduce labour costs, to identify the effects which such reductions may have not only on a specific sector, but on the economy as a whole.

Greater productivity may reduce employment in one sector, and at the same time create additional real income which should normally appear, at the macroeconomic level, in the form of higher wages, lower prices, or greater profits. The normal effect of increasing wages or lowering prices is to increase consumption. Greater profits are indispensable to the growth of investments which would in all probability occur if the right conditions existed in terms of global demand. The real income generated in one sector by investments which enable labour costs to be reduced should therefore help to increase demand and, consequently, employment in other sectors.[15]

Furthermore, technological developments and the capital/labour substitution to which they give rise should allow workers to be progressively redeployed in new jobs (programming of robots, social employment, etc.). Although automation in fact significantly reduces direct labour costs, it requires the support of an increasing number of related services (maintenance, inspection, preparation, organisation). Jobs with low skill content will therefore give way to employment requiring a higher level of skills.

High labour costs and an artificially low cost of capital are liable to encourage investments of marginal utility, leading to some waste of capital. The restoration of a balance between such costs would make these investments unprofitable and perhaps have a beneficial effect on employment. But in this case, only the least useful investments should be discouraged, namely those which are profitable only because they are supported by general or specific measures designed to encourage investment and because certain employers' contributions artificially swell the cost of labour. However, attempts to lower the wage bill by reducing the size of employers' contributions must, as will be seen below, be limited to those contributions which can be considered an unjustified tax on employment, namely those which are used to finance benefits completely unrelated to the guarantee of income from employment.

In any event, given the current international economic context, the industrialised countries should, if foreign trade is to remain the cornerstone of their economies, look to the possible reduction of their labour costs in terms of encouraging, rather than discouraging capital/labour substitution.

The problem of labour-intensive enterprises

Does the use of wages as the sole base for the assessment of employers' contributions discriminate between enterprises by penalising those which are labour-intensive in comparison with those which are highly mechanised? Such penalisation is generally appraised in terms of the share represented by employers' contributions in the value added; [16] this share in fact varies quite considerably from sector to sector, according to their degree of mechanisation. This explains why it has frequently been proposed that employers' contributions should be based not only on wages but on the entire value added.

It will be shown that it is less at the level of a country's different sectors of activity than at that of enterprises within the same sector that discrimination can really be said to exist. It will also be pointed out that such discrimination cannot be attributed to employers' contributions as a whole, but only to those used to finance benefits which are not designed to ensure a guaranteed income from employment.

As regards employers' contributions based on wages, it is not really possible to say that discrimination exists at the sectoral level, and this, for at least three reasons.

In terms of competitivity, it cannot be said that employers' contributions impose a burden on the least mechanised sectors which puts them at a disadvantage in comparison with sectors which are on the contrary highly mechanised. Production in the different sectors is, in fact, very different and therefore not competitive.

As regards profitability and dynamism, employers' contributions do not appear to exert any significant influence. The results of a simple econometric study covering approximately 50 sectors of the French economy show in this connection that the ratio between employers' contributions and value added (an indicator of possible discrimination) has no significant influence on either profitability (the ratio between the net result of operations and net position or fixed assets) or an enterprise's self-financing capacity (the ratio between cash flow and net position or fixed assets) in these different sectors.[17] The sectors with the highest ratios are not necessarily those which obtain the worst results; nor are those with the lowest social charges the most profitable or dynamic. Similarly, a study carried out in France [18] stresses that labour-intensive industries (defined in terms of total staff costs as a component of value added) form a very mixed group, which includes not only low-wage sectors which have to compete with highly competitive foreign enterprises but also competitive advanced-technology industries requiring a high level of skills. Thus, sectors such as glass, engineering or transport equipment are well placed in relation to national average productivity (measured by per capita value added) and economic performance (measured by the increase in net production between 1970 and 1976 and by the contribution of the trade balance to the domestic market between 1974 and 1976).[19]

Finally, although employers' contributions are, in all probability, generally incorporated in cost and selling prices, capital-intensive sectors using a small labour force make "indirect" contributions, namely contributions included in the cost of the raw materials, equipment and energy they need for their production.[20]

Labour-intensive enterprises which operate with little machinery will probably be more sensitive to contributions based only on the wage bill. Within the same sector, small- or medium-sized firms (which are often the most labour-intensive) may thus appear to be penalised in comparison with larger enterprises which are generally more mechanised. But this is not enough by itself to justify broadening the contribution base to include the whole of the value added.

First, capital-intensive enterprises using many machines have their own specific burden of energy, maintenance and equipment replacement costs. It would therefore be dangerous, as will be explained below, to reduce the social charges of labour-intensive enterprises by increasing those of capital-intensive enterprises.

Secondly, not all employers' contributions should be systematically considered as unjustified charges on employment. Everything depends on the conditions governing the provision of the benefits such contributions finance. It is only when contributions are paid for the financing of benefits unrelated to the exercise of an occupational activity (family benefits, medical care, minimum old-age pensions, grants for handicapped persons, etc.) that they can be said to constitute an unjustified charge on employment, but in such cases only. The most logical solution to such a situation appears to be to replace them by greater recourse to taxation.[21] As regards contributions earmarked to finance benefits, or part of benefits, which are themselves calculated on the basis of income from employment, there is no reason to criticise the fact that they are calculated on the basis of wages. They are part of the normal cost of labour, a form of *deferred wages* which workers do not receive direct, but which are paid globally to the social security organisations.

The imposition of a ceiling on contribution

The imposition of a ceiling is rightly often blamed for making employers' and workers' social contributions degressive in relation to wages and thereby accentuating the disparities between incomes and social conditions.[22] It also tends to have a negative influence on the level of employment.

Employers' contributions

It is undeniable that the placing of a ceiling on employers' contributions limits the social charges borne by wages above this ceiling and may therefore appear likely, at first sight, to encourage recruitment. Generally speaking, however, such a ceiling seems, on the contrary, to act as a brake on employment.

First, it is an incentive to the use of a small labour force; it reduces the number of offers of part-time jobs and encourages firms to lengthen the working day rather than recruit more staff, when the overtime payment is above the ceiling.

Secondly, the ceiling begets discrimination between high and low wages. It restricts the growth of the latter by making any wage increase more difficult for employers to finance. It therefore tends to restrict the growth of consumption by the social categories with the highest propensity to consume and has, therefore, a negative influence on the level of employment.

Finally, by limiting the contribution base, the application of the ceiling means that for a given amount of receipts, higher rates will be applied than would have been the case in the absence of any limitation to the base. The ceiling can therefore be said to increase artificially the cost of unskilled labour and curb recruitment by firms needing such labour. Assuming unchanged total charges, the removal of the ceiling would mean lower contribution rates with a corresponding reduction in the social charges on wages below the ceiling. In this way, it would therefore help to remove the obstacle to the recruitment of unskilled labour often constituted, in the eyes of employers, by its high cost price.

Workers' contributions

The application of a ceiling to contributions paid by workers and self-employed persons means that the percentage of the charges on their income will decrease in inverse proportion as this income rises. Since workers with low incomes are those with the greatest propensity to consume, and workers with high incomes are those who have the least propensity to consume, the ceiling, through its anti-redistributional effect, tends to reduce the average propensity of the entire population to consume, and hence has a restrictive effect on demand and employment.

The purpose of the first part of this chapter is to examine the validity of the criticisms which are most frequently made of the effects on employment of contribution systems based on wages. Some of these criticisms are no doubt excessive, but the exploration of various solutions which may enable social security financing methods to exert a more positive influence on employment is nevertheless a subject which merits attention.

POSSIBLE SOLUTIONS

Before examining various possible reforms, two important remarks should be made.

The first is that the possible scope of such reforms as a means of combating unemployment should not be exaggerated. Unemployment is in effect the result of many factors, and the high cost of labour (which itself has little connection with the role played by the social charges of enterprises in such costs) is only one aspect of the problem.

The second remark is that new financing methods should not be sought for purely economic reasons, however legitimate such arguments may be. It is certainly very desirable, in the continuing economic crisis, to identify which receipts are least likely to weaken growth, accelerate inflation and discourage employment. However, such an approach should not disregard the social objectives of each benefit and make social security financing simply an instrument of economic policy. It should, on the contrary, be set in a wider context, with a view to achieving greater harmonisation between financing sources and the nature of the benefits and the methods by which they are provided. Respect for this logical criterion should be the starting point of any attempt to rationalise the financing of social security. [23] It is, in any case, a prerequisite to the identification of the financing methods that are the least prejudicial to the operation of the economy. If financing is indeed based on logical criteria, it will no longer be possible to accuse it of being a brake on employment.[24]

It is from this standpoint that most of the proposals for modifying the way of calculating contributions will be rejected in the following pages and that preference will be given to the solution based on recourse to taxation (the replacement of certain contributions by the proceeds of taxation). But it will also be shown that as regards benefits which in some countries are already financed by taxation or which, in other countries, should logically be financed by it, the question of the relationship between social security financing methods, labour costs and employment is one which concerns the general structure of the taxation systems currently in force.

In the second part of this chapter, consideration will therefore be given to the following three possibilities: new methods of calculating contributions; recourse to taxation; and the structural modification of taxation systems.

In each case, the volume of expenditure to be financed will be taken as given. Since the purpose of this study is limited to examining the impact of social security financing methods on labour costs and employment, the argument will be based on the assumption that the level of charges remains unchanged. The analysis will therefore only be concerned with the advisability of adopting provisions for the transfer of charges between highly mechanised enterprises (broadening the contribution base to include elements other than wages, the establishment of contributions based on amortisation payments or the application of differential contribution rates in respect of firms or sectors); or between low-wage and high-wage enterprises (raising or removing the ceilings on contributions); or between high-income and low-income households (removal of ceilings on contributions paid by wage earners and self-employed persons; the financing of certain benefits from taxation); or between enterprises and households (reduction of employers' contributions offset by higher taxation of households).

New methods of calculating contributions

These may include the application of differential contribution rates by enterprise or sector, the broadening of the contribution base to include the whole of the value added, the establishment of contributions based on amortisation payments, or the removal of the ceiling on wages subject to contributions. In each case, the aim would be to reduce disparities resulting from contributions based solely on earnings or from the application of a ceiling on contributions. With the exception of the last-mentioned hypothesis (the removal of the ceiling), these various directions for reform concern, above all, employers' contributions.

Differential contribution rates

This proposal is based on the calculation of such disparity indicators (between sectors or firms) as the ratio of staff costs or employers' contributions to added value or employers' contributions to staff costs. It would consist in the application of reduced contribution rates to sectors or firms where the selected disparity indicator is higher than the national average and, conversely, the application of higher rates to sectors or firms where the indicator is lower than the national average. The process is thus designed to stop penalising labour-intensive sectors or firms and, in cases where contributions are subject to a ceiling, those in which a large proportion of the wages is below the ceiling.

However, whether applied at the level of the sector or the firm, this proposal is not without its defects.

The application of a *sectoral corrector coefficient* to contribution rates has two major drawbacks. First, it means treating all firms belonging to the same sector in the same way, whereas the disparities which separate firms in the same sector may well be greater than those which exist between specific sectors. Secondly, the inclusion of an enterprise in any given sector depends upon its principal activity. An enterprise which carries on several kinds of activity would therefore be subject to the application to its entire range of activities of a uniform corrector coefficient which would be determined in accordance with its principal activity.

As a remedy for these drawbacks, it has also been proposed that a *corrector coefficient* should be applied *by enterprise*. However, whatever ratio may be used to calculate this coefficient, the various formulae obtained would always tend to make the collection of contributions excessively complicated and increase the operating costs of social security.

Generally speaking, this kind of solution is, above all, envisaged as a means of avoiding recourse to taxation or the removal of the ceiling on contributions. It would undoubtedly tend to reduce the charges borne by capital-intensive enterprises which employ a high percentage of unskilled labour; but it would also give rise to many more technical difficulties and, above all, would do nothing at all to adapt financing methods more closely to the nature of the benefits provided.

Broadening the contribution base to cover value added

Under this proposal, the basis for employers' contributions would no longer be restricted to wages alone, but would be extended to include as well financial costs, amortisation and profits (if the total contribution remained the same, broadening the base would imply a reduced rate of contribution). This formula should not therefore be confused with recourse to the indirect taxation technique known as the value added tax (VAT). There are in fact two basic differences between these two systems.

The value added which is proposed as a wider base for employers' contributions corresponds to the difference between actual production and intermediate consumption. Contributions levied on such a base would thus apply to all goods and services produced, irrespective of whether they are sold or retained in the enterprise. They are neutral in respect of the utilisation of production factors, since they are levied on both wages and amortisation. The VAT base, on the other hand, is much narrower and does not cover goods or services exported, goods held in stock or, most important, amortisation. It is therefore not neutral in respect of the utilisation of production factors, since it is not levied on investments. From this point of view, some writers argue that the effects of VAT are similar to those of employers' contributions based solely on wages.[25]

Even if the cost of contributions based on the entire value added is finally incorporated into the selling price, such contributions increase the charges borne by enterprises, in contrast to VAT which is borne directly by the final user, since this tax is levied only when the transaction takes place. Employers' contributions based on the entire value added would therefore only result in a transfer of charges from labour-intensive enterprises to highly mechanised ones, whereas a reduction in employers' contributions combined with an increase in VAT rates would result in lower global charges on wages for all enterprises, and in particular for labour-intensive ones.

According to those who have suggested that the contribution base should be broadened to include the entire value added, such a formula would have three advantages as regards employment.[26]

First, it would abolish the discrimination in the choice of production factors in favour of capital and against labour which results from contributions based on wages. Employment would be promoted in as far as the reduction in the relative cost of labour vis-à-vis the cost of capital would encourage enterprises to make a greater use of the former.

In the same way, such a system would abolish any discrimination between highly mechanised and labour-intensive enterprises. By improving the situation of the latter, it would exert a positive effect on employment.

Finally, by reducing the cost of labour, this system would extend the useful life of equipment, since the latter would remain profitable longer. This would in turn reduce replacement investment and make it possible to increase exports.[27]

Broadening the base of employers' contributions to the entire value added is, however, a formula with defects that are serious enough to warrant its rejection.

First, such a measure would not reduce the global share of the enterprises of a country in the financing of its social security. It would result only in a *transfer of charges* from labour-intensive to highly mechanised enterprises. It is extremely difficult to gauge the exact overall impact of such a transfer since analysis could not be restricted simply to variations in social charges from sector to sector or even from enterprise to enterprise,[28] but would also have to take account of their direct or indirect repercussions on wages, prices, self-financing and investments in each sector and then, at the global level, on the main economic variables and, in particular, on the level of employment.

Such analysis presupposes not only the use of extremely detailed multisectoral, macro-economic models, but also the formulation of several alternative hypotheses on the ways in which enterprises react to modifications (whether upward or downward) in the level of their social charges. This in turn involves the difficult *problem of measuring the incidence of social charges borne by enterprises*, that is to say identifying who would bear the real burden or who would benefit in real terms from possible increases or reductions in the contribution rate or base.[29] Higher contributions may affect a firm's self-financing capacity and/or distribution of profits. The extra burden may, however, be passed on to wage earners in the form of lower wage increases, or to consumers, if it is incorporated in cost or selling prices, or to the public authorities and thence to taxpayers as a whole, if greater support (subsidies, tax relief) has to be given to some enterprises.

The incidence of a change in the base of employers' contributions is thus far from being uniform. It is related to multiple factors (such as a firm's profit goals, its degree of exposure to foreign competition, the form and intensity of competition on the markets for its products, the nature of its production factors, the supply and demand elasticities of its products, trade union strategies and the policies of the public authorities) which make it extremely difficult to gauge its impact on any given variable of economic activity. This helps to explain why major differences occur in the interpretation of the expected effects of any given reform of financing methods. But it should above all encourage the public authorities and social partners to direct their reform projects towards the search for a coherent and logical relationship between each type of benefit and the financing method best adapted to the objectives sought and the kind of solidarity provided.

At the purely economic level, the broadening of the base of employers' contributions to the whole of the value added runs the risk, contrary to the forecasts of those who support such a policy, of having an adverse influence on economic growth and the level of employment. It would penalise investments by imposing a double burden on them: upstream, in terms of the running costs for the manufacture of capital goods and downstream, in the amortisation of their cost. Furthermore, profits would also be affected, as part of the value added. Such a measure would thus be liable to slow down the modernisation of the production process, which would have pernicious repercussions on economic growth, industrial competitivity and in the end, on employment.

A recent Belgian study has simulated, on the basis of the MARIBEL macro-economic model, the effects of broadening the base of employers' contributions to the entire value added (on the assumption that the contribution yield remained unchanged).[30] The results showed that such a policy would lead to a reduction in the charges based on wages which would in turn slow down the rate of inflation. The increase in the cost of capital utilisation would, on the other hand, directly reduce investment to a very marked extent, which would entail a slowing down of growth that would wipe out completely the potentially positive effect on employment of the reduced inflation rate. In short, such a policy would on the whole have a negative effect on growth and employment.

It is symptomatic that another study on the same subject but in relation to the French economy, reached different conclusions.[31] The hypothesis which was tested by simulations carried out with the DMS (dynamic-multisectoral) model was that of a reduction, in 1977, of employers' contributions levied on wages by 10 percentage points (the average rate for the year in question being reduced from 34 per cent to 24 per cent of wages), compensated by the establishment of a new contribution of 3.5 per cent levied on value added (but not deductible for exports). The study showed that such a measure would have made it possible to create 180,000 jobs in six years.

The DMS model used in this study is a multisectoral model and as such, more suited to this kind of simulation than the purely global MARIBEL model used for the Belgian simulation.[32] There is considerable uncertainty, however, concerning the conclusions of the French study. The latter, in effect, assumes that enterprises benefiting from the lightening of their social charges as a result of the measure under consideration would pass on the entire alleviation in correspondingly smaller increases in their selling prices, so that, for the same contribution yield, despite the effect of the increased contributions borne by highly mechanised enterprises, a "marked decline in inflation" would be obtained. This conclusion is too optimistic. First, the enterprises benefiting from such reductions would in all probability not pass on the full amount of the relief in their prices; secondly, the sectors most affected by this extension of the contribution base would include such basic industries as gas, electricity, petroleum and fuel. Such reductions would therefore have induced effects on production costs in other sectors.[33] In the same way, the French study carried out by the General Planning Commissariat does not take account of the indirect effects of variations in social charges incorporated in intermediate consumption and capital equipment goods.[34]

The repercussions and macro-economic effects of broadening the base of employers' contributions to the entire value added are thus very uncertain. For economies based to a large extent on foreign trade, and in the current international economic context, such a broadening policy may well prove prejudicial to the most dynamic undertakings and hinder industrial redeployment by slowing down technological progress and leading to a decline in industrial productivity and competitivity.[35]

A measure of this kind would also prove very unfair to individual enterprises which, although they employ no wage earners, would still have to pay employers' contributions. As the French study by the General Planning Commissariat points out, these enterprises could of course be excluded from the scope of the new system; however, should the same policy apply to small enterprises which operate with only a few wage earners? Would the recruitment of only one or two persons be sufficient to require an enterprise to pay social contributions on the whole of the value added which it creates? The case of individual enterprises is not only important in itself, but illustrates, at a more general level, the profound ambiguity created by the dissociation of employers' social contributions from the employment of wage earners.

It is clear from the foregoing that the broadening of the base of employers' contributions to include the whole of value added is, in fact, a form of taxation. However, as will be seen in the following pages, not all employers' contributions should be replaced in this way, and other taxation methods would undoubtedly have a more positive influence on employment.

Establishment of contributions based on amortisation

This formula is designed to offset the effects of contributions based solely on wages by extending the burden to the factor of capital. The supporters of the system maintain that it would encourage employment since it would make it possible to apportion social charges more equitably between enterprises and thus no longer penalise labour-intensive enterprises in comparison with those which are highly mechanised.[36]

The only advantage of this system over the formula of contributions based on value added appears to be that it does not penalise the profits of enterprises (which are already subject to corporate tax or personal income tax, as appropriate). Apart from that, however, it would penalise enterprises which make efforts to invest and would also, once again, separate employers' contributions from the employment of wage earners. As in the case of the previous system studied, it fails to promote any closer adaptation of the financing methods to the calculation methods applicable to each benefit.

Removal of the ceiling on contributions

The gradual removal of the ceiling on employers' and workers' contributions, accompanied by a reduction in contribution rates, would first establish greater social justice, since contributions would then be proportional for all wages, irrespective of their level. From the point of view of employment, the removal of the ceiling could likewise have an impact that would be the greater the lower the ceiling (or ceilings in systems which comprise several different ceilings according to the branches, or the persons protected) in relation to average wages, and the larger the share of contributions based on wages subject to a ceiling in total social security receipts.

The removal of the ceiling on contributions paid by wage earners and self-employed persons would improve the redistributional effect of social security. By increasing contributions paid by workers with high incomes and reducing those of workers with low incomes, it would increase the propensity to consume of the entire community and would have a positive effect on employment.

The removal of the ceiling on contributions paid by employers would be an incentive to the use of part-time employment and encourage employers to have less recourse to overtime rather than engage supplementary labour. Such a measure would also lighten the charges affecting the employment of unskilled labour. Assuming an unchanged total contribution yield, the removal of the ceiling on employers' contributions would in effect result in a transfer of charges from firms employing a large amount of unskilled labour remunerated below the ceiling to firms which, on the contrary, require highly skilled workers whose wages are above the ceiling. It may be feared that the latter firms, which often belong to dynamic sectors very vulnerable to foreign competition, would thus be penalised in respect of their self-financing capacity or cost prices and, consequently, their competitivity, but the extent of such a risk has to be appraised in the light of two sets of considerations.

For firms in high-wage sectors, an increase in their compulsory contributions would not necessarily have a negative effect on their recruitment projects. Indeed, it is quite possible that since employers' contributions are basically a form of deferred wages, the effect of an increase in the contributions levied on high wages would be to limit the growth of the latter and thereby, to some extent, narrow the range of wages. It is equally conceivable that the increase of compulsory charges could be offset by a reduction in employers' contributions to conventional and voluntary protection systems, which are often more developed in the high-wage than in the low-wage sectors.

It is above all in terms of the nature of the contributions and benefits that the removal of the ceiling must be justified. The ceiling was originally designed to exclude wage earners whose earnings exceeded the ceiling from the benefits of social insurance; there is thus no justification for retaining the ceiling in a social security system that covers all wage earners, particularly when it involves certain economic and social drawbacks. Thus, there is no logical reason to fix a ceiling for contributions which are designed to finance cash benefits providing replacement income (sickness or unemployment benefits, pensions, invalidity benefits) and therefore really appear to be a form of deferred wages. The same applies to contributions which finance benefits designed to guarantee minimum social standards (sickness-insurance benefits in kind, family benefit, basic unemployment benefit and benefits for elderly persons in need). The question of the removal of the ceiling on such contributions should, however, be subsumed in the more general question of the replacement of such contributions by financing from public funds, namely taxation.

The removal of the ceiling on some contributions, accompanied by the replacement of other contributions by recourse to taxation, could therefore under certain conditions (which are specified below in the section on taxation) reduce the labour costs of all firms, including those which employ highly paid personnel.

Any measure to remove the ceiling on contributions is, however, likely to give rise to acute dissatisfaction and lead to very delicate political problems, since it will tend to strengthen the redistributional effect of social security. Furthermore, if such a measure were undertaken in isolation and on a uniform basis, it would not be appropriate for all the branches of social security. A decision to remove the ceiling should thus form part of a wider reform based on principles of equity and congruity [37] and designed to adapt the financing and calculation methods for each benefit to its specific nature and the solidarity mission projected for it.[38]

Recourse to taxation

The replacement of some contributions by recourse to taxation is a measure which, under certain conditions specified below, would make it possible to base the financing of the benefits in question on sources more appropriate to the nature of the benefits and at the same time act as a stimulus to employment by lightening the burden of charges affecting labour costs.

Why taxation?

The real justification for the use of taxation is above all a matter of principle. The arguments involved concern the countries whose systems were initially based on the German legislation of Bismarck, and have since evolved towards the broadening and generalisation of their objectives.

With the extension of systems initially designed to protect only wage earners to include persons who are not wage earners and to persons who do not exercise an economic activity, the systems have in effect ceased to be essentially commutative, based on work and the notion of insurance, and have acquired a more distributive character in which greater emphasis is placed on the duty of society towards the satisfaction of the basic needs of its members.[39] There is therefore no longer any reason to continue to levy contributions based only on income from employment, when the benefits they finance are extended to social categories which do not receive any such income. The proposal to use taxation therefore concerns those branches where benefits are in fact an expression of national solidarity and in which there appears to be no logical relationship between contributions based on income from employment and the benefits which such contributions are used to finance.

What should be taxed?

This question calls for the identification of two distinct major categories of benefits, and the clarification of the significance today of social contributions as a whole and of the distinction between contributions paid by wage earners and contributions paid by employers.

A distinction should be made between two major categories of benefits: earnings-support benefits and benefits designed to guarantee certain minimum social standards.[40]

Recourse to contributions based on income from employment is logical only within the framework of solidarity strictly related to the field of insurance; in other words, when benefits, too, are calculated in proportion to the income they are designed to guarantee. The right to such benefits is linked to the exercise of an economic activity. Such persons are therefore obliged to make an effort to provide for the future. Contributions, whether from workers or employers, thus represent a part of the wage which the insured person does not receive directly but which is used to guarantee cash benefits in support of earnings during periods of forced inactivity (old age, sickness, invalidity, unemployment).

On the other hand, the granting of minimum social benefits to the entire population is invariably based essentially on the ideas of social assistance or national solidarity. In such cases, recourse to taxation is the most appropriate financing method, since there is no relation between the benefits granted and the beneficiaries' income from employment. Benefits such as the provision of medical care or the reimbursement of medical costs, family benefits or basic allowances granted to elderly persons in need should therefore be financed from public funds.

Benefits designed to guarantee income from employment which include both a uniform basic component and the payment of a sum calculated in proportion to earnings, come under the heading of both national solidarity and insurance (pensions and unemployment benefit schemes clearly illustrate this phenomenon, since they are often in effect designed to guarantee on the one hand, minimum means of subsistence equal for all and on the other hand, the maintenance of a certain level of living based on previous income from employment). As is moreover often the case, they should be financed on a joint basis. Only the part calculated in relation to earnings should be financed by contributions; the other part should come from taxation. The respective size of these two parts is a political choice. It is bound up with the recognised rights of beneficiaries as members of the economically active population and as members of the national community.

This distinction based on the type of solidarity provided by each benefit helps to clarify the significance of social contributions. At the economic level, social contributions, as compulsory charges, can be regarded as a category of taxes. However, it follows from the above that the term "contributions" should be restricted to charges which constitute a form of insurance, are calculated in proportion to income from employment and entitle beneficiaries to benefits which are also calculated in proportion to income from employment.

The distinction between employers' contributions and workers' contributions assumes that the burden of the former is borne by the workers whilst the actual cost of the latter is effectively paid by the employer. Although the question of incidence has already been mentioned and will not be re-examined here, it seems clear that such a distinction is in the final analysis almost meaningless. It can be equally well maintained that both contributions are borne by wage earners or by employers.

It can, indeed, be argued that the burden of both contributions is borne by the insured person, because if the employer did not pay either his or his workers' contributions to social security, he would be able to increase net wages by the same amount, without increasing his cost prices. In the same way, it would be just as logical to argue that it is the employer who in fact bears the burden of both contributions since what matters for his production costs and competitivity is the total cost of his labour; the way this cost is divided between direct wages and social contributions is of no consequence. Workers' contributions can themselve be regarded as a charge on the enterprise, since their removal would allow a corresponding reduction to be made in production costs without affecting the available income of the wage earner.

This question is in fact closely linked with the co-existence of the ideas of insurance and national solidarity in social security systems, and with the related question of the nature of employers' contributions. Should the latter be regarded as a kind of deferred wage (a fraction of the wage paid direct by the employer to the social security organisations on behalf of the wage earner) or as a tax levied for the purposes of financing public service organisations?

The answer to this question is simple once it is recognised that the contribution system should be used only to finance the guarantee of income from employment. There is thus no reason to calculate employers' contributions other than on the basis of the wages which such contributions are designed to guarantee. They are indeed an integral part of the normal cost of labour and constitute a deferred wage, which is not received directly by the wage earner but is paid in to the social security organisations on his behalf. Moreover, the international systems of national accounting record employers' contributions as operating costs to be included in the wage bill.

From this point of view, the distinction between workers' contributions and employers' contributions becomes practically meaningless. It would be more logical, instructive and practical to group the two contributions in a single contribution corresponding to that part of the wage which is compulsorily assigned to the guarantee of the latter.

Problems involved in taxation

The main problem—the choice of the taxes to be used—will be examined in the following section. However, before attention is given to the choice of appropriate taxation methods, other problems need to be examined. These concern above all the increase in tax pressure, the possible reform of the administration of some social security organisations and the option between budgeting and "taxation" in the strict sense of the term.[41]

Increases in the burden of taxation may well be resented by taxpayers. Of course, there is no reason why the total receipts from compulsory social contributions and taxes taken together should be substantially modified since the process involves only a simple substitution between the two forms of charge. For insured persons, however, contributions are less painful since they are deducted at source and are partly financed by enterprises. Most insured persons also prefer to see a direct link between contributions and the benefits to which they know they are assigned. Thus, it would undoubtedly be necessary to adopt a system of progressive taxation in order to upset insured taxpayers as little as possible and, by means of adequate information, make them conscious of the need for solidarity.

Should the *administration of the social security bodies*, where this is the responsibility of the insured persons, be called in question on account of the transfer to taxation of the financing of certain benefits because the system of contributions based on income from employment appears to be better adapted to the principle of joint management (by employers' and workers' representatives)? This does not appear to be indispensable since management methods are not necessarily connected with financing methods.[42] Irrespective of the source of financing, it is indeed conceivable that the public authorities would not directly take on the day to day management, leaving this to the insured persons, but would reserve for themselves the control of legislation and regulations. In this way each fund could receive credits calculated on the basis of the number and age groups of its members.

The choice between budgetary financing and financing through taxation properly so-called depends upon whether the benefits financed by taxation should be covered by budgetary receipts as a whole or by recourse to special taxes. Two kinds of arguments are sometimes put forward in favour of taxation proper. First, given the structure of taxation systems and the widespread practice of tax evasion and fraud, it is not certain that budgetary financing would be more equitable than financing from contributions. Secondly, the irregularity of some budgetary resources and the risk of their being contested each year by Parliament, would hardly be compatible with the essentially unavoidable nature of social security expenditure.

These arguments are not really convincing. Although it is true that some tax systems still appear to be unfair, there is no *a priori* reason to assume that greater justice will be served by taxation rather than budgeting. Both options involve an increase in tax pressure and in both cases the choice of the taxes to be increased or created could provide the authorities with an opportunity for restructuring the tax system in a way deemed to be more in keeping with social justice.

Fears regarding irregularity in the credits allocated to social security each year are undoubtedly exaggerated. Social security expenditure is no more unavoidable than most other sectors of public expenditure (general administration, national defence, education, etc.) and if the State does not wish to increase taxation, it can always resort to loans to increase receipts. It is by no means certain that the imposition of special taxes is any more reliable than budgeting. Once it is admitted that certain social benefits are a national solidarity commitment, and should therefore be financed wholly or partly by taxation, they can justifiably be considered as genuine public expenditure.

STRUCTURAL MODIFICATION OF TAXATION SYSTEMS

General principles

As regards benefits or parts of benefits which, according to the country concerned, are already covered or should logically be covered by taxation, the question of the method of financing them raises the more general question of the structure of the taxation system in force in the country concerned. It is in fact the financing methods of public expenditure as a whole–and not only those of social benefits covered by taxation–which should be adapted to the various economic and social goals pursued by the authorities. At a very general level, the objective of taxation should be to finance public expenditure in the most equitable and least uneconomic manner possible. These two criteria are, however, very relative, since they depend upon political, economic and social choices which vary according to the country, period and circumstances involved. Thus, the definition of what is equitable depends upon the political choice of a "desirable" wage structure and the objectives to be assigned to the public finances as regards the reduction of disparities in income and social conditions. As for the economic criterion, this is at the present time related to the basic emphasis laid by most of the market economy industrialised countries on adapting their production to the new conditions in the international division of labour. In the light of this objective, the least uneconomic taxes are those least likely to have repercussions on labour costs and affect the self-financing capacity of enterprises.

From this point of view, if social security financing methods are to help to improve industrial competitivity and employment without lowering the level of social protection, or to allow increases in social security expenditure to be met without undue prejudice to industrial competitivity and employment, the direct income of households must be limited. For this solution to be viable, three conditions are required: in countries where contributions are used to finance benefits unrelated to the guarantee of income from employment, such contributions must be replaced by taxation levied on households; within the overall tax system, the tax burden on enterprises must be lightened and heavier taxes placed on households; any increase in the tax burden on households must be accompanied by measures designed to set or limit the level of prices and wages so as to prevent any corresponding increase in the cost of labour.

The taxes to be increased or created could be chosen and imposed in such a way as to place a greater burden on the rich. They would then strengthen national solidarity and at the same time increase the average propensity of the entire population to consume.

The choice of taxes to be imposed

The tax increases (or new taxes) to be imposed must be those least likely to exert upward pressure on direct wages. Any increase in compulsory charges tends to encourage claims in respect of wages, since householders are above all concerned with their real available income (purchasing power); that is to say, they are conscious of changes in prices and the compulsory charges they have to bear but fail to appreciate fully the advantages they obtain from public expenditure. This explains the tax-push inflation phenomenon which affects industrial costs, particularly during the negotiation of wages.

Increased taxation of goods and services is a possible solution, but one which must be used with considerable caution.

Generalised use of value added tax (VAT) (either the creation of such a tax or an increase in the rate, according to the country) may appear to be an attractive taxation method from the point of view of employment, since imports would be taxed but exports exempt. Such a measure would therefore assist exports and allow a larger portion of social security charges to be passed on to goods manufactured abroad, in particular cheap goods imported from countries with low labour costs. However, the use of VAT also involves risks which must be clearly borne in mind.

First, any taxation measure based on VAT is likely to accelerate inflation and increase the upward pressure on direct wages. VAT is in effect a tax which is included in selling prices; the financing of workers' contributions by such taxation would therefore affect prices. As regards the replacement of employers' contributions by such a tax, prices would remain unchanged only if firms passed on the entire reduction in their wage costs to their selling prices before tax. In this case alone, the drop in prices before tax would be exactly equal to the rise in VAT. It would therefore only be necessary for some firms to take advantage of their reduced labour costs to increase their self-financing or distribution of profits–rather than reduce their prices–for the replacement of employers' contributions by taxation to be itself fuel to inflation. Thus any decision to reduce employers' contributions compensated by recourse to VAT must be accompanied by sufficiently effective price control measures to avoid appropriation of the reduction by the firms.[43] In this case, the reduction in labour costs resulting from lower employers' contributions would not increase a firm's self-financing and investment capacities.

According to GATT regulations, VAT is deducted from the price of goods which are exported, but is applied to goods which are imported. The use of VAT to cover employers' contributions could therefore make it possible to increase employment in export enterprises (the reduction in labour costs, uncompensated by VAT, would allow them to choose between a reduction in their prices and an increase in their profits) and in enterprises which are exposed to strong foreign competition on the domestic market (by raising the price of imported goods).

As regards foreign trade, the compensation of reduced employers' contributions by VAT appears to be a protectionist measure tantamount to devaluation. It would therefore on the one hand, be liable to lead to the phenomenon of imported inflation (increase in the price of exports with the risk of successive repercussions on prices as a whole), and on the other hand, to be viewed as a dumping measure and as such, be resented by the trading partners of any country pursuing such a policy.

Finally, VAT is a tax which is open to criticism from the point of view of social justice, since it affects all consumers equally and takes no account of their contributive capacity. It even tends to be degressive as income increases, since low wage earners, whose propensity to consume is greater than that of high wage earners, are proportionally more subject to the tax. The application of differential rates on the basis of the utility of products is not sufficient to make the effects of VAT progressive in relation to income.

It merely makes it possible to limit the regressive impact of the tax in question.

As far as taxes on goods and services are concerned, preference should be given to increasing taxation on luxury goods, and on forms of consumption and activities generating substantial expenditure on medical care: alcoholic beverages, tobacco, motor vehicles, equipment required for activities considered to be dangerous, etc.

The increase of personal income tax is a solution which appears attractive for several reasons.

Public revenue statistics (taxation plus social charges) for OECD member countries [44] show that the countries which have most recourse to contributions for the financing of their social security expenditure are generally those with the lowest income tax (see table 12). The processing of these statistics by the factorial analysis of correspondences [45] has even indicated that the basic differences between the taxation structure of these countries can be simply expressed in terms of their recourse which varies from country to country–to either social contributions or income tax. Taxation in the form of personal income tax would therefore promote some degree of harmonisation between these different tax structures, since the countries which currently make the most use of contributions would be those with the most reason to resort to taxation.

Personal income tax is levied on all incomes and is graduated according to earnings. In respect of the equitable distribution of the tax burden, its effect is therefore exactly the opposite of that of contributions based solely on income from employment subject to a ceiling.

Finally, such taxation would be very likely to encourage employment. First, its progressive structure makes it more redistributive than contributions paid by wage earners and self-employed persons; by replacing such contributions, the tax therefore tends to increase the propensity of the entire population to consume and so to stimulate demand and employment. Secondly, since its base is much wider than that of contributions (particularly when these are subject to a ceiling), a reduction in the rate of the latter can be compensated by a smaller increase in income tax rates. The replacement of workers' and employers' contributions by taxation, which will increase net wages and reduce labour costs will, although it increases the income tax burden, be likewise less liable to have repercussions on wages and prices than the imposition of a general tax on goods and services.

Recourse to income tax must, however, be accompanied by a real attempt to combat tax evasion and fraud, which reduce the tax yield, often to a considerable extent. In some countries, the base could also be broadened and some of the calculation methods could be modified so that the increase in yield would not depend solely on an increase in rates. For example, the following measures might be considered: the inclusion in the tax base of family benefits or workers' contributions used to finance earn-

Table 12.   Structure of compulsory charges in OECD member countries, 1978
(Percentages)

Country	Personal income tax	Corporate tax	Social security contributions	Property tax	Taxes on goods and services	Other charges
Australia	43.71	10.64	–	8.88	31.39	5.38
Austria	23.76	3.18	30.57	2.91	31.60	7.98
Belgium	34.96	5.96	30.02	2.80	26.13	0.13
Canada	32.65	11.41	11.75	10.00	32.24	1.95
Denmark	51.01	3.16	1.34	6.11	38.25	0.13
Finland	44.15	4.30	10.30	2.29	38.96	–
France	13.13	4.66	42.04	3.33	31.27	5.57
Germany (Fed. Rep. of)	29.89	5.79	33.90	2.95	26.05	1.42
Greece	10.70	4.06	28.04	12.18	43.91	1.11
Ireland	28.64	5.00	13.73	5.88	46.64	0.11
Italy	20.48	8.84	40.71	3.68	26.28	–
Japan	21.95	18.41	29.49	8.56	17.24	4.35
Luxembourg	26.54	21.40	28.47	5.15	17.63	0.81
Netherlands	26.43	6.27	37.30	4.13	25.62	0.25
New Zealand	59.38	7.98	–	8.73	23.40	0.51
Norway	36.55	4.87	17.98	1.77	37.94	0.89
Portugal	10.96	.	29.76	1.48	38.02	.
Spain	18.30	5.44	49.50	5.15	21.39	0.22
Sweden	42.16	3.05	26.73	0.83	23.76	3.47
Switzerland	36.34	6.34	29.75	7.19	20.38	–
Turkey	39.16	4.40	15.02	5.45	31.17	4.80
United Kingdom	33.79	7.18	18.33	12.19	26.54	1.97
United States	34.49	11.40	25.03	12.10	16.97	–

. Figure unknown. – Negligible.
Source: OECD: *Revenue statistics of OECD member countries 1965-1979* (Paris, 1980).

ings support benefits, the replacement of the family quota in respect of dependants by a system of fixed rate tax reductions, the revision of the methods used to calculate various tax reductions and exemptions, etc.

An increase in property tax is another possibility, in so far as this tax generally accounts for only a small part of total compulsory charges (table 12). Increasing the tax on property transfers or the creation or increase, as the case may be, of a permanent property tax, are methods which, if certain precautions are taken, would not seriously risk increasing prices and wages.

An increase in corporate tax would probably be passed on to the consumer (through higher prices) or else prejudice industrial investment capacity. Moreover, under GATT regulations, corporate tax, unlike VAT, is not deductible from export prices. An increase in this tax would therefore risk jeopardising industrial competitivity. Furthermore, with the growth of international trade and the multinationalisation of production, corporate tax is especially vulnerable to evasion and fraud at the international level and these are extremely difficult to control. Too much hope cannot therefore be placed on increasing the scale of this tax.[46]

The foregoing considerations regarding various possible taxation methods do not claim to be exhaustive. Their chief purpose has been to show that the financing of certain social benefits by means of taxation can be justified on logical grounds and should, if it is to contribute at the same time to the solution of the problem of unemployment, be based on a genuine policy of national solidarity.

A real attempt to rationalise the budgetary options covering the whole range of public expenditure could also be envisaged. This would perhaps facilitate a better identification of priorities and enable real economies to be made on certain items of expenditure, whose usefulness is not always examined with sufficient care.[47] A larger share of resources from taxation could then be made available for social security financing.

CONCLUSIONS

The main purpose of this chapter has been to highlight the complexity of the mechanisms whereby various alternative methods of social security financing can influence employment. Less attention has therefore been paid to finding a miracle solution than to illustrating the multiple economic and social aspects of a problem which is of crucial importance today, at a time of declining economic growth, high inflation, widespread unemployment and increasingly keen international competition, when many countries are finding it difficult to cope with the rise in their social security costs.

To this end, the problem has been viewed in terms of the option chosen by most of the market economy industrialised countries to accentuate industrial redeployment and intensify international specialisation. It was, however, considered that it would be dangerous to try to use social security as a vehicle of economic policy, since its specific objective should, above all, be that of providing social protection.

In an area where arguments and counter-arguments are legion, preference has therefore been given to the identification of the financing methods best adapted to the kind of solidarity implemented by each category of benefit, the level of these benefits and the conditions under which they are provided being essentially the result of political options and economic constraints.

This approach has made it easier to delimit the respective spheres of taxation and contributions, and to specify under what conditions the latter can be considered a normal labour cost. If financing methods are thus established on rational bases, there will no longer be any justification for accusing the contribution system itself of being an obstacle to employment.

This does not, however, prevent the public authorities from providing assistance to certain enterprises by granting subsidies taking over the payment of part or all of their contributions.

It is therefore only in relation to the taxation system as a whole and the volume of the sums levied to finance the various categories of social benefits that the problem of labour costs and their impact on employment can be properly stated.

As regards the choice of the taxes to be imposed to finance all or part of the benefits unrelated to the guarantee of income from employment, the objective must be to harmonise economic imperatives with requirements of equity. The former are currently determined by the trend in most of the Western industrialised countries to accentuate the international division of labour and promote a more integrated world economy.

It is in relation to this objective, the validity of which is moreover open to question—but that is another subject—that the attempt has been made in this chapter to determine which taxes would be the least likely to exert a negative influence, either directly or indirectly, on labour costs and, consequently, on industrial competitivity and employment.

Notes

[1] A tax system, strictly speaking, may be defined as one which covers all public receipts, excluding social security contributions, as opposed to a tax system broadly understood as a system of compulsory charges, including the social contributions to which wage earners, employers, independent workers and inactive persons are liable.

[2] In this connection, see in particular H. Grubel (ed.): *The effects of unemployment insurance on unemployment* (Vancouver, Simon Fraser University, 1980). The longer period of time spent looking for a job may, on the other hand, facilitate closer matching of workers' qualifications with required skills, and thus promote manpower stability.

[3] In this connection, see in particular E. Malinvaud: *The theory of unemployment reconsidered* (Oxford, Basil Blackwell, 1977).

[4] J. Fayolle: "L'attitude des entreprises face à la concurrence étrangère", in *Economie et statistique* (France, Institut national de statistique et d'études économiques), Aug. 1980, p. 64.

[5] The survey carried out in June and July 1980 by the International Chamber of Commerce and the IFO-Munich Institute in 950 enterprises in 45 countries shows that labour costs are now the most important factor determining the increase of production costs. In the same way, the report of the European Management Forum: *Report on the competitiveness of European industry* (Geneva, 1980) points out that of the ten main factors used in the report, the "industrial efficiency and production costs" factor is the one which is the most heavily weighted and that labour costs are the principal component of production costs.

[6] A. Bienayme: *Stratégie de l'entreprise compétitive* (Paris, Masson, 1980), p. 90.

[7] This paragraph reproduces part of an article by A. and Ch. Euzéby: "Sécurité sociale, coût de la main-d'œuvre et compétitivité des entreprises", in *Revue d'économie politique* (Paris), Sep.-Oct. 1981.

[8] Identical observations can be made for each industrial branch in the different countries of the European Economic Community (EEC). Comparative statistics are available for the level and structure of production costs in the different industrial branches in these countries. An analysis of these statistics shows that there is no connection between the percentage of

social charges in labour costs and the size of the latter. On this point, see in particular A. Euzéby: "A propos des cotisations sociales patronales", in *Droit social* (Paris), Apr. 1977, pp. 113-121.

[9] See in particular OECD: *Public expenditure trends* (Paris, 1978), Annex B, pp. 81-87; J. Pitchford and S. J. Turnosky: "Some effects of taxes on inflation", in *Quarterly Journal of Economics* (Cambridge, Massachusetts), Nov. 1976, pp. 523-539; D. A. L. Auld: "The impact of taxes on wages and prices in Canada", in *National Tax Journal* (Columbus, Ohio), No. 1, 1974, pp. 147-150; J. Johnson and M. C. Timbrell: "Empirical tests of a bargaining model of wage rate determinants", in *Manchester School of Economic and Social Studies* (Manchester), No. 2, 1973, pp. 141-167; R. J. Gordon: "Wage-price controls and the shifting Phillips curve", in *Brookings Papers on Economic Activity* (Washington, DC, Brookings Institution), No. 2, 1972, pp. 385-421.

[10] Among the measures introduced by different countries, reference may be made to: the replacement of taxation on production by a value added tax deductible from capital goods; free, degressive or accelerated depreciation schemes; tax deductions for investment; tax incentives to savings; scientific and technological research, exports, national development; taxation schemes governing the merger and integration of enterprises, etc. In this connection, see in particular B. Bobe and P. Llau: *Fiscalité et choix économiques* (Paris, Calmann-Lévy, 1978); G. Kopits: *International comparison of tax depreciation practices* (Paris, OECD, 1975); J. Wiseman and M. Davenport: *Theoretical and empirical aspects of corporate taxation* (Paris, OECD, 1974).

[11] According to a French study (E. Malinvaud: "Peut-on mesurer l'évolution du coût d'usage du capital productif?", in *Economie et statistique* (Paris), Apr. 1971), the combined effect of VAT, depreciation systems and tax deductions for investment resulted in a 23 per cent drop in the cost of capital utilisation between 1949 and 1969.

[12] In this connection, see in particular V. Woodward: "The pattern of final demand and the sectoral composition of employment in the United Kingdom, 1963-1980", in OECD: *Structural determinants of employment and unemployment*, 2 vols. (Paris, 1977 and 1979).

[13] Between 1970 and 1979, this percentage rose from 17 per cent to 25.6 per cent for manufactured products as a whole (from 8 per cent to 39 per cent for cars, 51 per cent to 99 per cent for office material and from 51 per cent to 90 per cent for data-processing equipment (see V. Keegan: "The spanner in industry's works", in *The Guardian* (London), 21 Jan. 1980)).

[14] This idea found no support moreover amongst the participants in the Experts' Meeting on Employment Problems which was organised by the OECD in Paris in March 1977. See *Structural determinants of employment and unemployment*, op. cit., and J. R. Gass: "Structural determinants of employment and unemployment: Commentary on a meeting of experts", in *OECD Observer* (Paris), July 1977, pp. 31-35. The experts did not exclude the possibility that governments may have encouraged the introduction of "heavy" prestige equipment without giving sufficient attention to its economic efficiency, at the expense of "light" and adaptable equipment requiring the use of a larger human element. In such cases, however, it is not technological progress as such which is open to criticism, but rather excessive and insufficiently profitable investments.

[15] Commission of the European Communities: *Investment and employment*, doc. II/795/77 (Brussels, 1977), p. 25.

[16] In this connection, see in particular N. H. Douben: "Sociale premiedruk; een gevarieerde last", in *Social maandblad Arbeid* (Alphen an den Rijn, South Holland), No. 7, 1976, pp. 424-434; H. Deleeck, M. De Decker and J. Huybrechs: "Financiering van de sociale zekerheid door bijdragen berekend op de toegevoegde waarde der Belgische ondernemingen in plaats van op het loon", in *Cahiers économiques de Bruxelles* (Brussels), No. 72, 1976, pp. 451-477 and No. 73, 1977, pp. 57-59; M. A. Frank: "Substitution de la valeur ajoutée aux salaires comme base de calcul des cotisations des employeurs à la sécurité sociale", in *Cahiers économiques de Bruxelles*, No. 72, 1976, pp. 437-448; C. de Neubourg and H. Caspers: *Social security system financing: charges on the net value added and other alternatives in the Netherlands*, Memorandum (Institute of Economic Research, Faculty of Economics, University of Groningen, 1980) published in *Cahiers économiques de Bruxelles*, No. 93, 1982. See also the study carried out in France by the Economic and Social Council: "Problèmes posés par le mode de calcul des cotisations sociales, notamment au regard des industries de main-d'œuvre" (Boutbien report), in *Journal officiel de la République française*, Avis et rapports du Conseil économique et social (Paris), No. 12, 1974, pp. 663-680.

[17] A. Euzéby: "A propos des cotisations sociales patronales", op. cit., pp. 113-121.

[18] Commissariat général du Plan: *L'assiette des charges sociales et les industries de main-d'œuvre*, Rapport au Premier Ministre (Paris, 1977).

[19] ibid., pp. 14-16.

[20] The amount of contributions contained in intermediary consumption and gross fixed capital formation in the various sectors of French economy has been calculated by the Division of Social Studies of the Forecasting Directorate of the Ministry for the Economy and Finance. The figures show, for example, that in the petroleum sector–where costs account for a small part of the value added–approximately 90 per cent of employers' contributions are levied indirectly (ibid., p. 31).

[21] However, recourse to taxation does not necessarily result in a reduction of labour costs. As will be seen below, such a reduction requires recourse to a form of taxation which is the least likely to result in an increase in wages.

[22] In this connection, see in particular J. A. Brittain: *The payroll tax for social security* (Washington, DC, Brookings Institution, 1972); H. Deleeck: *Maatschappelijke zekerheid en inkomensherverdeling in Belgie* (Louvain-Antwerp, Centrum voor economische studiën, Standaard Wekenschappelijke Uitgeverij, 1966); idem: "Sociale zekerheid en inkomensherverdeling", in *Economisch en Sociaal Tijdschrift* (Antwerp), No. 4, 1975, pp. 403-420; "Sécurité sociale et distribution des revenus", in *Reflets et perspectives de la vie économique* (Wezembeek, Brabant), No. 4, 1976, pp. 297-310; J. J. Dupeyroux: *Droit de la sécurité sociale*, op. cit.; A. and C. Euzéby: "A propos du plafond des cotisations de sécurité sociale", in *Revue d'économie politique* (Paris), No. 6, 1980, pp. 833-844; H. J. Krupp: "Verteilungswirkungen der Steuerfinanzierung des sozialen Altersversicherungssystems", in B. Külp and W. Stützel (eds.): *Beiträge zu einer Theorie der Sozialpolitik* (Berlin, Dunker und Humblot, 1976); A. Munnel: *The future of social security* (Washington, DC, Brookings Institution, 1977), Ch. 5; F. Pavard: "Social security financing through the contribution method", and J. H. Petersen: "Financing social security by means of taxation", in *Methods of financing social security*, Studies and Research, No. 15 (Geneva, International Social Security Association, 1979), pp. 13-24 and 25-60.

[23] On the various elements of such rationalisation, see the article by G. Perrin: "A propos du financement de la sécurité sociale", in *Revue belge de sécurité sociale*, op. cit., pp. 769-791. See also Chapter 5 below.

[24] In this case the negative effect of high labour costs on employment may be ascribed only to direct wages and/or the level of social security.

[25] Artus, Sterdyniak and Villa: "Investissement, emploi et fiscalité", in *Economie et statistique*, op. cit., pp. 119-120.

[26] In this connection, see in particular the report of the committee set up in France at the request of the Ministry of Social Security to study the reorganisation of the contribution base (Granger Report) (Paris, 1975), pp. 8 ff.; M. De Decker: "De differentiele weerslag van de loongrens op de loonkost in de onderscheiden productiesectoren", in *Economisch en Sociaal Tijdschrift*, No. 6, 1976, pp. 887-892; H. Deleeck: "Un autre mode de financement de la sécurité sociale: des cotisations calculées sur la valeur ajoutée", in *Reflets et perspectives de la vie économique*, No. 3, 1977, pp. 191-199; and *Droit social*, Nos. 9-10, Sep.-Oct. 1977, pp. 340-342; Deleeck, De Decker and Huybrechs: "Financiering van de sociale zekerheid door bijdragen berekend op de toegevoegde waarde der Belgische ondernemingen in plaats van op het loon", op. cit.; Douben: "Sociale premiedruk; een gevarieerde last", op. cit.; and *Sociale zekerheid, een economische benadering* (Deventer, Kluwer, 1979); Frank: "Substitution de la valeur ajoutée aux salaires ...", op. cit.

[27] In this connection, see B. Mourre: "Aspects économiques d'un changement d'assiette des cotisations sociales", study by the Forecasting Directorate of the Ministry for the Economy and Finance (Division of Social Studies), in *Statistiques et études financières* (Paris), Orange Series, No. 32, 1978, pp. 44-52; also the article by J. P. Launay: "Financement de la sécurité sociale et politique économique", in *Droit social*, Jan. 1981, p. 75.

[28] For the present purpose, "direct" social charges are those which are paid directly by enterprises to the social protection organisations. "Indirect" social charges are those which are borne by an enterprise as a result of the direct charges which are passed on to it in its purchase of capital goods and intermediate consumption needed for its production. At the branch level, indirect charges can be evaluated by the use of input-output tables.

[29] Empirical studies and theoretical analyses have failed to give a really satisfactory

answer to the question of the incidence of employers' contributions. They have moreover resulted in contradictory conclusions. In this connection, see J. A. Brittain: "The incidence of social security payroll taxes", in *American Economic Review* (Nashville, Tennessee), Mar. 1979, pp. 110-125; M. S. Feldstein: "The incidence of the social security payroll tax: Comment", in *American Economic Review*, Sep. 1972, pp. 735-738; J. H. Leuthold: "The incidence of the payroll tax in the United States", in *Public Finance Quarterly* (Beverly Hills, California), Jan. 1975, pp. 3-13; W. Vroman: "Employer payroll tax incidence: Empirical tests with cross-country data", in *Public Finance* (The Hague), No. 2, 1975, pp. 184-200; J. Weitenberg: "The incidence of social security taxes", in *Public Finance*, No. 2, 1969, pp. 193-208; D. Hamermesh: "New estimates of the incidence of the payroll tax", in *Southern Economic Journal* (Chapel Hill, North Carolina), Apr. 1979, pp. 1208-1219.

[30] P. Huge: *Simples propos sur la sécurité sociale et sur son financement* (Brussels, Bureau du Plan, 10 Feb. 1981), p. 32.

[31] Commissariat général du Plan: *Assiette des charges sociales . . .*, op. cit.

[32] On the use of models in social security studies, see Coppini and Laina, op. cit.

[33] Similarly, other studies show that a broadening of the base of employers' contributions to the whole of the value added would lead to a transfer of charges between enterprises which would seriously affect the more mechanised sectors, as well as sectors (such as agriculture, business), which comprise a large number of small individual enterprises employing few or no wage earners. Thus, in the case of Belgium, according to calculations made by Frank, op. cit., table 1, for the year 1970 such an extension would increase contributions by 141.2 per cent in the oil products sector; by 110.7 per cent for electrical energy; by 99.9 per cent for water (piping, filtering, supply); by 195 per cent for maritime transport; by 35.5 per cent for iron ore and ferrous metals, etc. . . . Similar calculations have been made, in particular by Deleeck, De Decker and Huybrechs, op. cit., for Belgium and by Douben, op. cit., and de Neuboure and Caspers, op. cit., for the Netherlands.

[34] The authors of the report point out in this connection that the INSEE DMS model used in this simulation does not incorporate a sufficiently detailed sectoral breakdown to take account of these indirect effects, which are, however, very important (see table 6, p. 31 of the report).

[35] Coppini also points out that social security financing methods which are likely to discourage technological progress should be avoided, since the mechanisation of numerous production processes is beneficial to the entire community (see *The problems involved in social security financing*, Note No. 2 (Brussels, Commission of the European Communities, doc. V/1351/77), p. 6).

[36] See in particular the articles of M. Huguenot: "Plaidoyer pour une idée saugrenue: la taxation des amortissements comme mode de financement de la sécurité sociale", in *Droit social*, Feb. 1973, pp. 53-57 and Frank, op. cit. The second author in fact recommends the establishment of contributions based on both wages and amortisation payments.

[37] On these principles, see M. A. Coppini: *Problems of social security financing*, Note No. 3 (Brussels, Commission of the European Communities, doc. V/173/78-FR).

[38] A. and C. Euzéby: "A propos du plafond des cotisations de sécurité sociale", op. cit.

[39] In this connection, see in particular the articles by G. Perrin: "La sécurité sociale au passé et au présent", op. cit., and G. M. J. Veldkamp: "L'extension de la protection sociale aux catégories de personnes autres que les travailleurs: dynamique de l'Etat-providence et relations industrielles", in *Droit social*, Apr. 1977, pp. 108-112.

[40] Similar proposals can be found in particular in Dupeyroux: *Droit de la sécurité sociale*, op. cit.; R. Boelaert: "Modes alternatifs de financement de la sécurité sociale: une analyse de différentes propositions", in *Revue belge de sécurité sociale*, Feb. 1979, pp. 117-132; A. Druan Heras and B. Gonzalo Gonzalez: "Alternativas para la reforma financiera de la seguridad social", in *Prespuesto y gasto público* (Madrid), No. 7, 1980, pp. 57-73; A. Euzéby: "Faut-il fiscaliser la sécurité sociale?", op. cit.; Munnel: *The future of social security*, op. cit.; Instituut voor sociaal Zekerheidsrecht: *Ontwerp van Wetboek Sociale Zekerheid* (Louvain, Universitaire Pers, 1978), pp. 120-134; V. Scotti: "La fiscalizzazione degle oneri sociali e il contenimento del costo del lavoro", in *Sicurezza sociale oggi* (Rome), No. 5, 1979, pp. 75-92.

[41] On these points, see in particular A. Euzéby: "Faut-il fiscaliser la sécurité sociale?", op. cit.

[42] Thus in France agricultural social security funds are managed by the insured persons themselves, although their resources come essentially from taxation.

[43] In the United States, the Advisory Council on Social Security recently unanimously adopted a recommendation that the share of contributions in social security receipts should be reduced. But it rejected–also unanimously–the use of VAT because of the inflationary risks involved. See *Social security financing and benefits*, Reports of the 1979 Advisory Council on Social Security (Washington, DC, United States Department of Health, Education and Welfare, Dec. 1979).

[44] *Revenue statistics of OECD member countries 1965-1979* (Paris, OECD, 1980).

[45] G. Gilbert: *Economie politique des structures fiscales*, doctoral thesis, University of Paris X, 1979.

[46] In this connection, see in particular A. Margairaz: *La fraude fiscale et ses succédanés* (Lausanne, 1970); G. W. Holmes and J. L. Cox (eds.): *Tax fraud* (Ann Arbor, Michigan Institute of Continuing Legal Education, 1973); and G. F. Kopits: *Taxation and multinational firm behaviour: A critical study*, IMF Staff Papers, No. 3 (Washington, DC, 1976).

[47] Of the numerous studies on the methods of rationalising public expenditure options, see in particular R. H. Haveman and J. Margolis: *Public expenditure and policy analysis* (Chicago, Rand McNally College Publishing Company, 1977); L. Weber: *L'analyse économique des dépenses publiques: fondements et principes de la rationalisation des choix budgétaires* (Paris, Presses universitaires de France, 1978); P. A. Pyrrh: *Zero-base budgeting: A practical management tool for evaluating expenses* (New York, J. Wiley and Sons, 1973); and J. S. Wholey: *Zero-base budgeting and program evaluation* (Lexington, Toronto, Lexington Books, 1979).

NATIONAL EXPERIENCE OF FINANCING

4

This chapter contains a description of social security financing experience in six countries (Argentina, Australia, France, Hungary, Spain and the United States). Although this description brings out certain common problems—especially the need to meet a continuous general increase in expenses in very difficult economic circumstances—it also highlights the importance of specific features of national schemes. For example, the structure of financing differs greatly from country to country. In Australia the system is financed mainly from public revenue, whereas in France, Spain and the United States social security has been traditionally financed by means of wage-based contributions. In Argentina a similar structure obtained until 1980, when the employers' contributions were replaced by a fraction of value added tax (VAT). In Hungary—as in many countries with centrally planned economies—financing by means of wage-based contributions is being increasingly supplemented by state subsidies. In all countries changes are—or have recently been—under discussion. But because of national characteristics, and especially the weight of tradition, as well as the principles on which social protection is based in each country, the future of financing raises different problems from one country to another.

This chapter is based on the national monographs submitted to the ILO Meeting of Experts on Social Security Financing and reflects the main points made in them. The monographs were written by Mr. Amancio C. Lopez, Director General of the Office of Sectoral Development, Secretariat of State for Social Security (Argentina); Mr. Colin McAlister, First Assistant Director General, Development Division, Department of Social Security (Australia); Mr. F. Pavard, Director of the National Old-Age Insurance Fund for Employees (France); Mr. T. Farkasinszky, Assistant Chief of the Department of Social Policy, Ministry of Labour (Hungary); Mr. J. Velarde Fuertes, Professor, University of Henares, Madrid (Spain); and Mr. Robert J. Myers, the then Deputy Commissioner of Social Security Programmes, Social Security Administration (United States).

CHANGES IN METHODS OF FINANCING IN ARGENTINA

Before 1980 the Argentine social security system was financed for the most part by means of contributions from workers and employers. In July of that year, on the proposal of the Ministry of the Economy, the Government decided to do away with the employers' contribution (15 per cent of wages, plus 5 per cent in the form of a contribution to the National Housing Fund) and to replace it by an equivalent sum obtained from an increase in value added tax (VAT). Strictly speaking, the contribution from public funds by which it was decided to compensate the loss of the employers' contribution was to have been drawn from tax revenue as a whole and not from an earmarked percentage of VAT, but in point of fact the rate of VAT was increased to cover this new charge on public funds.

The decision was motivated, in principle, by the belief that such taxation, being more neutral than the employers' contribution, would have certain advantages for the whole economy. It was particularly designed as a means, in the prevailing economic situation, of reducing production costs in order to compensate industry for the effects of a monetary policy that was artificially maintaining the parity of the peso with the US dollar.

Implementation of the new measure raised a number of problems. The first of these was how to determine the size of the compensatory subsidy. At the outset, the subsidy, which was equal to the contribution that had been abolished (namely 15 per cent of all wages subject to contribution), represented a given percentage of total tax revenue. It had to be decided whether that percentage should serve as the invariable basis for calculating the subsidy, and if so, whether that did not involve a risk that the social security scheme would one day run short of resources.

The level of social security expenditure fluctuates with trends in wages (since the law links benefits to the wage index); but whereas the former employers' contributions also varied proportionately with wages, the same is not true of tax-based resources, which–particularly in the case of VAT–follow prices. As a result, either the adjustment of benefits in step with wages had to be abandoned, or a formula not based on a predetermined fixed percentage had to be found for the calculation of the share of taxes to be earmarked for social security.

The choice fell on the second solution, not merely so that the revaluation of benefits could continue but also for technical reasons: the payment of benefits has a seasonal rhythm different from that of taxes; with a fixed percentage the resources of social security would depend on the capacity of an institution outside the system to collect revenue on its behalf.

The formula adopted consisted in the calculation of the subsidy every month on the basis of the contributions actually collected from wage earners.

Another problem was to preserve the autonomy of the social security system in general and particularly in connection with the collection of funds. To this end, a scheme was first evolved that would have left the structure of the collection system intact. Broadly speaking, the employers' obligations towards the system would have been maintained: they would have continued to pay their contributions as before but would have been able to deduct them from their payments under VAT (at the increased rate). Labour-intensive firms would therefore have been able to deduct more than capital-intensive ones, which would have made it possible to achieve the desired goals without interfering with the social security mechanisms.

But the scheme was dropped and a way had therefore to be found to ensure the autonomy of the system in the collection of funds. It is no secret that Treasury Departments sometimes go through difficult periods, when the funds to be transferred to social security are liable to constitute a serious temptation. To avoid this danger, it was decided that the National Bank, which collects all revenues on behalf of the Ministry of Finance, should effect the transfer before the funds were paid to the Treasury. As a further precaution, the law authorised the social security authorities to issue drafts on the National Bank so that it need not wait for the transfer to be made in order to have funds at its disposal.

There still remained one major problem. What would happen if the National Bank was at any time unable to honour a draft because its amount was larger than the total of all taxes collected? To meet such a situation, it was decided that the draft would be backed by the Central Bank, the only institution capable of covering the deficit.

The safeguards adopted have proved effective. So far the flow of funds has not been interrupted and the social security scheme has operated without a hitch. Certain fears remain, however. As time goes by the beneficiaries of the measure adopted may well "forget" that VAT was increased so that their production costs could be lowered by 20 points, and it would then not be surprising if theorists were to cite the pressure of taxation as a ground for the reduction of public expenditure, of which social security would, quite unjustifiably, be regarded as a part. Things would have been different if the proposal to maintain employers' obligations towards the scheme had been adopted.

FINANCING THE AUSTRALIAN MINIMUM INCOME SUPPORT SYSTEM

Social security in Australia comprises a number of separate but sometimes overlapping schemes run by the Federal Government, or by the State or territorial governments, or by voluntary commercial insurance. The most important of these schemes, and the only one to be considered here, is the minimum income support scheme provided by the Federal Government (Department of Social Security). Supplementing this scheme is, first, a compensation for work-related injuries and deaths under which benefits are provided by the several states. Based on the principle of employer responsibility it takes the form of compulsory commercial insurance; employers' premiums are risk-related. Some of the workers are covered by voluntary retirement pension schemes operated through commercial insurance and financed by premiums paid by the insured persons and/or their employers with the support of special federal tax concessions. A health care system run by the Federal Government (supplemented by agreements concluded with the various state governments) and financed from public funds, provides basic medical and hospital care for lower income groups. Voluntary commercial insurance for health costs, financed by individual premiums supported by special tax concessions, is available to the remainder of the population. A system of cash payments and health care for war veterans and their families is financed from public funds. Finally, mention should be made of other welfare benefits in cash and in kind granted by local authorities, the states and the Federal Government, as well as income replacement payments, provided by employers under certain conditions, in case of sick leave. Approximately 13 per cent of Australia's gross domestic product (GDP) is at present devoted to social security.

The guaranteed minimum income support system is designed to provide persons unable to work, prevented from working or who cannot find work (the aged, handicapped, sick, sole parents, the unemployed) with uniform, taxable cash benefits, short- or long-term as the case may be. Except for persons over 70 years of age, these benefits are subject to an income test. Entitlement ceases above a given level of income (representing about 52 per cent of the average wage for single persons and 87 per cent for married couples); below these thresholds, benefits are inversely proportionate to income. Over the years the income test has been progressively liberalised. The system also provides universal, non-taxable family allowances for all dependent children. It is financed entirely from public funds. Its cost represents 6.7 per cent of GDP (6 per cent excluding family allowances) and its benefits reach 47 per cent of the population (22 per cent excluding family allowances).

The use of public revenue financing for this system—which, it must be remembered, is the most important element of social security in Australia —reflects in part the Government's anti-poverty aims. In this context, financing cannot be considered in isolation from benefit structure: it is considered that the payment of income-tested, flat-rate benefits financed from general revenue is conducive to greater "target efficiency" than earnings-related social insurance, because the poverty alleviation is greater for a given level of expenditure.

The question arises, however, whether financing by means of contributions would not be productive of more funds—and hence provide a larger sum to be spent on the alleviation of poverty—than general revenue financing. It is difficult if not impossible to answer this question. It appears that the social insurance approach could indeed provide greater resources–how much greater is uncertain–but the redistribution of the increment to the needy is more problematic in view of the psychological importance of maintaining a close link between contributions and benefits. If taxable capacity is sufficient to obtain more funds through contributions, then it would not be unreasonable to conclude that a large part of that capacity would make it possible for taxation to be increased. In that case, the whole of the difference could be allocated to the most needy on the basis of social priorities rather than contribution record.

In a guaranteed minimum income system, the level of benefits paid has to be taken into account in assessing the degree of poverty alleviation. The flat-rate benefits provided by the Australian system do not necessarily imply a low level of earnings replacement rates. On the contrary, for low income earners they can be quite high, especially if higher pensions are paid to married couples and in respect of dependent children. Nor should fringe benefits, such as free health care, be overlooked. Higher earners can obtain higher income replacement rates through private insurance (especially through subsidised occupational pension funds), but this involves contributions on the part of the earner or his employer, or both.

The Australian system has the additional advantage of catering better for the needs of classes of persons who have never been attached to the labour force or whose elegibility has lapsed (the handicapped from birth, new entrants to the labour force, unmarried mothers, the long-term unemployed). For these persons, general revenue financing facilitates equality of treatment. For example all sole parents in Australia are eligible for minimum income support under the same conditions, irrespective of how they came to sole parenthood.

The general public revenue financing system permits significant administrative simplification by avoiding the need of complex machinery for the calculation and collection of contributions, as also for the calculation of benefits on the basis of past contributions. Administrative problems may be erected by the application of the income test, but the basic assessment processes are mechanical and straightforward.

Another advantage of a public financing system is that it is more readily adaptable to the global requirements of state fiscal and monetary policy, especially during economic recession. Because social security expenditure tends to be more flexible under general revenue financing, owing to the absence of quasi-contractual promises, the government runs less risk of being bound by commitments that it may not in some circumstances be able to honour (even though the scope for cutting back social security expenditure may be rather circumscribed owing to the political difficulties that may result). Finally, in as far as general revenue financing involves a more progressive tax structure, the system tends to be self-stabilising: revenue will rise more quickly than incomes when economic growth is strong, less so when growth is weak.

Nevertheless, pressure is periodically brought to bear in support of basic changes in the structure and financing of the system, and particularly for the introduction of some form of financing by contributions.

In 1938 legislation was passed by the Federal Parliament to provide for a compulsory social insurance system restricted to wage earners, levying flat-rate contributions and paying flat-rate benefits; but the legislation was not implemented for a number of reasons. It was felt that social insurance would not overcome poverty among the aged or those unable to contribute or excluded from the scope of the scheme (notably farmers and other self-employed people). Wage earners considered that they should not be obliged to contribute directly; they viewed the contributions as a "sectional" tax that disregarded the capacity of the individual to pay. Employers feared that such a system would generate pressure for higher wages and thereby reduce profitability. Finally, the state governments considered the system to be an intrusion into areas, such as workmen's compensation, that were and still are their responsibility.

In 1945 a contributory National Welfare Fund was nevertheless established. All government health and social services expenditure was paid from the Fund, which was financed by a "social services contribution" (that is, an earmarked tax additional to income tax), a payroll tax and a contribution from the Government. By 1952, the social services contribution had been merged with general income taxation and the Fund had become a mere accounting device.

In the field of health care, an indirect link between contributions and benefits was reintroduced in 1976. The new system of health care (Medibank) introduced for the whole population in 1974 was originally to have been mainly financed by a levy of 1.25 per cent of taxable income and a government subsidy but, failing the necessary legislation, it was financed entirely from general revenue. Contributions were again introduced in 1976: insured persons could choose between receiving benefits under the Medibank scheme, in which case they paid a levy of 2.5 per cent of taxable income (with ceilings), or contributing to approved private health insurance funds. In 1978, however, the levy was abolished in connection with other changes in the health care system.

During the 1970s two bodies of inquiry recommended the introduction of contributory schemes. First, the National Commission of Inquiry into Compensation and Rehabilitation (1974) recommended a national scheme providing automatic and universal coverage for all injured and sick people. One of the aims of this scheme was to remedy the inadequacies of the existing schemes relating mainly to their basis in common law. Benefits under the scheme were to have been earnings-related, payable without regard to income and consistent with benefits under the minimum income support system. The scheme was to have been financed by a payroll tax on employers and a sales tax on petrol. Legislation to implement the scheme (limited, however, to accident insurance) was introduced in 1974, but it lapsed with the change of government the following year.

The Inquiry into National Superannuation also recommended (1976) the introduction of a contributory scheme. The scheme, which was free of any means test, would have provided a universal pension, an earnings-related purchased pension and a supplementary pension for people whose purchased pension did not reach a certain minimum level. A compulsory contribution of 5 per cent of income would have financed the purchased pension as well as a small part of the universal and of the supplementary pensions; the balance would have been made up from general revenue. The inquiry thought that higher priority should be given to increasing the general level of pensions rather than to providing large pensions to people with high pre-retirement incomes. But it considered that some degree of earnings-related benefits was also needed if the contributions were not to be seen merely as an increase in income tax.

The Government did not adopt these recommendations. It felt that, even if contributions were linked to earnings-related benefits, they would be widely viewed as an additional income tax, whereas its general policy was to reduce the tax burden on individuals. Besides, the compulsory nature of the scheme was contrary to the Government's view that individuals should be free to choose the form in which they saved. Finally, the Government wanted to direct assistance towards the most needy, and feared the imbalance that would have resulted from age pension rates higher than the levels of other benefits.

Unlike the two inquiries mentioned above, the Poverty Inquiry (1975) favoured a scheme entirely financed from general revenue, constituting an adaptation of the existing minimum income support system. In the proposed scheme, categorical income support payments would have been replaced by a general guaranteed minimum income based on a poverty line. To finance the scheme the Government was to levy a proportional tax on all private incomes. These recommendations were not adopted in their entirety, but they led to certain improvements in the existing system (means test replaced by a test on income only, tax deductions for children replaced by family allowances, etc.).

* * *

In Australia, as in many other countries, it has been asked whether the current system is viable, since the growth in outlays seems to be outstripping the community's capacity (and willingness) to pay through taxation. The question arises whether other methods of financing social security would not be better able to cope with likely future demands on the system. Between 1970 and 1980 social security and welfare outlays grew at an average annual rate of 22 per cent (10.5 per cent in real terms), increasing from about 10 to about 27 per cent of the total expenditure of the Federal Government; but this proportion stabilised during the last four years of the decade. It must be pointed out that the increase was caused not only by demographic changes and adverse economic conditions but also by policy decisions to improve benefits.

Setting aside the last-mentioned factor, which is unforeseeable, the future costs of social security will be determined mainly by the growth in the number of aged people. Although Australia's population is slowly ageing, it is relatively well placed in this respect compared with other industrial countries. In 1980 about 11.7 per cent of the population were of pensionable age (65 and over for men, 60 and over for women). This percentage is expected to increase to about 13.7 by the year 2000. The ratio of aged to working-age people will increase from its present level of 18.5 per cent of 21.7 per cent by the end of the century.

On the other hand, the ratio of dependent children to active population should decline, which will result in a reduction of public–and above all private–expenditure on children. Hence the capacity of the working community to meet the increased costs of public expenditure should rise, the more so in view of the expected continuing rise in women's workforce participation rates.

Nevertheless, it is clearly economic growth that will be the crucial factor determining ability to meet future demands. Even if considerable rises in average tax rates are required, taxpayers will be the more ready to accept them if economic growth leads to a rise in their own net income.

Another issue is whether greater reliance on the private sector for income security can reduce the financing problems faced by the Government. This seems unlikely since, even though direct expenditure may be reduced, indirect costs such as tax concessions for participation in private pension funds would increase. Besides, from a macro-economic point of view social security expenditure is a burden on the economy, whether it is public or private.

Greater recourse to funding is sometimes envisaged in order to lighten the burden on future generations. But there is no real guarantee that greater funding will achieve that aim, and there is no reason why current transfers should not be based on current capacity to pay, so long as programmes do not involve unrealistic promises. In this respect, the Australian minimum income support system seems likely to avoid the difficulties that will have to be faced by social insurance systems financed by earnings-based contributions comprising a quasi-contractual element.

THE FINANCIAL EQUILIBRIUM OF SOCIAL SECURITY IN FRANCE

In France, as in the other countries of the European Economic Community, there has in recent years been a general and continuous increase in the share of social expenditure in gross domestic product. The breakdown of this expenditure is broadly similar in all countries. In contrast, the breakdown of financing varies widely from one country to another. In Denmark, for example, the contributions of the State and local communities represent about 84 per cent of the total, whereas in France it is less than 20 per cent.

In countries like France, where financing is based essentially on contributions, the relative shares paid by employers and workers are also highly variable.

During the period of economic growth that followed the Second World War social security expenditure in France increased at a rate that was nearly always higher than that of the production of wealth. Financial equilibrium was thus a recurring problem. At this point, however, the term "social security deficit", frequently appearing in the press, calls for closer consideration. There are, in fact, a number of aggregates which are often confused. The "social efforts of the nation" as set forth in the document annexed to the Budget Act do not have the same coverage as the "social protection account", which is not only part of the national accounts system but is also compatible with the European system of integrated social protection statistics. The global amount of these aggregates is of practically no significance, since it includes large amounts financed out of the state budget. The same applies to social security schemes as a whole, which are composed of many institutions, some of which, like the supplementary retirement schemes, are financially totally independent. In fact, the financial problems of social security mean basically the general scheme, in other words, the scheme for wage earners in industry and commerce.

The sharp rise in social protection expenditure (16 per cent of GDP in 1960, 27.3 per cent in 1980) was due to various factors that have often been analysed. Foremost among these are demographic factors (the ageing population, the trend towards a reduction in the length of working life, the attitude of women towards child-bearing and economic activity), which have long-term effects on the receipts and expenses of the old-age insurance scheme and indirectly on those of sickness insurance. Added to these are institutional factors (improvement of social coverage) which have more direct repercussions on costs, and economic factors which are decisive for general equilibrium.

Costs connected with unemployment have increased substantially since 1973. Besides receipts, a system almost 80 per cent of which is financed by contributions depends closely on economic activity and the number of contributors. The drop in resources due to the increase in unemployment was estimated at 30,000 million francs in 1980 for 1.5 million jobseekers.

It would, however, be wrong to attribute the financial difficulties of the social security scheme to unemployment alone. Between 1945 and 1974, a period of full employment, 11 increases were made in the global rate of contributions, which rose from 28 to 35.2 per cent, or by 7.2 points. During the same period, there were five decreases in the contribution rate for family allowances, which dropped from 16 to 9 per cent, or by 7 points. There were thus 16 changes in the rate, or more than one every two years, equivalent to an increase in the rate of 14.2 per cent for social insurance (sickness and old-age insurance).

In the past few years the expenses of the general scheme have risen by an average of 19 per cent per year, and receipts by an average of 12 per cent.

Rate adjustments had to be made in 1976, 1978, 1979 and 1980. They consisted in progressively raising the ceiling of the sickness insurance contribution (by 4 points in 1976 and by 9 in 1981) and increasing the rates for old-age insurance contributions (10.75 per cent in 1976, 12.90 at present). But it is obvious that a long-term disparity between receipts and expenditure will rapidly lead to an untenable situation.

When the Eighth Plan (1981-85) was being prepared the financial outlook for the social insurance schemes up to the year 1985 was calculated with the aid of models devised by the National Institute for Statistics and Economic Studies (INSEE) and the Forecasting Department.

This simulation, more than two years old, was based on economic hypotheses that now appear in some respects outdated. It assumes a drop in receipts followed at a later stage by a drop in expenses, and hence an aggravation of the financial imbalance of the social security system. It is further assumed that both legislation and behaviour will follow former trends, with two exceptions: measures are foreseen in favour of families and the rate of increase of supplementary retirement pensions will be checked. On the other hand, there will be no appreciable decline in the rate of increase of health care expenditure, and the projection does not contain any wishful thinking regarding the possibility of reducing expenses. The ceiling on contributions to the general scheme will be raised by 0.8 point per year, and the remaining deficit borne by the state budget. Contributions and the state subsidy to unemployment insurance receipts will increase in parallel.

According to this projection, the financial requirements of the social security schemes will be 50,000 million francs in 1985 (43,000 million for the general scheme). Unemployment compensation will cost the state budget 29,000 million francs (against 7,300 million in 1979), despite a steep rise in contributions (4 points for sickness insurance and 3.1 points for unemployment insurance).

As regards the breakdown of financing, it follows from the hypothesis adopted that the state contribution will increase substantially, the workers' contribution will remain stable, and the employers' contribution decline.

The short-term forecasts show a deficit of 7,000 million francs in 1981 and 23,000 million in 1982. Two phases have thus to be provided for.

Short-term measures have to be taken immediately to meet deficits in the coming months. In this connection, virtually the only possible solution is recourse to conventional measures: increasing contributions (the provisional increase of 1 per cent in the workers' contribution to sickness insurance, abolished in February 1981, might be reintroduced); raising the ceiling on the employers' contribution by a few points; reviewing the ceiling on contributions twice a year instead of once; increasing the contributions of certain categories (civil servants, the self-employed); and having the state budget take over all or part of the demographic subsidy.

In the longer term, more diversified measures are needed if lasting social security equilibrium is to be achieved. Four courses of action are usually suggested in order to remedy the financial imbalance: recourse to the state budget, a change in the base for contributions, abolition of the ceiling, and the absorption of unemployment.

The state budget grows more or less in step with GDP, whereas social security expenditure grows faster. Recourse to the budget cannot therefore be a lasting solution. Besides, it is impossible to raise the tax burden too abruptly: income tax would have to be raised by 60 per cent in order to cover transfer of family benefits.

Changing the base of contributions, in particular the inclusion of value added, was frequently discussed between 1974 and 1978. But there are technical difficulties. Firms where value added is high are first of all individual firms with few employees and their charges would be considerably increased; secondly, they are highly capital intensive, producing semi-finished products for use mainly by other enterprises whose costs would be consequently raised substantially. In this connection, the energy sector naturally comes to mind. Above all, the sum total of the value added by enterprises is precisely the commercial GDP, which raises the same problem as the preceding proposal.

As regards the abolition of the ceiling, the problem is whether the contribution system, which is at present regressive with respect to income, should be made proportional or progressive. The ceiling for the sickness insurance contribution has already been largely removed. Abolition of the ceiling for old-age insurance contributions would only be possible if measures were taken to safeguard the legitimate interests of supervisory staffs, whose supplementary retirement pensions scheme is financed on the basis of the fraction of their salaries above the ceiling.

Finally, the absorption of unemployment raises problems that no developed country has so far been able to solve. According to the report of the Committee on Social and Family Benefits for the Eighth Plan, only a small reduction in the number of unemployed would be obtained by a 6 per cent annual GDP growth rate. In the present international context no one believes in the possibility of a growth rate of that magnitude.

For 30 years the problem of balancing the social security budget has been posited mainly in terms of receipts and only subsidiarily in terms of expenditure. Yet this latter factor is essential.

A recent trend in economic thinking lays stress on the role of transfers in the creation of demand. Transfers can indeed provide remuneration for jobs in the health and social welfare sectors; they supplement inadequate incomes or make up for deficient wages. This creative role is not taken into account by macro-economic models, in which social policies are represented in terms of their cost and not of their yield. The principles of national accounting, which serve as a basis for global models, are partly responsible for this approach in so far as they take account of non-marketable services only in respect of their cost. This is the major shortcoming of cost/benefit studies, namely, that they quantify the non-marketable elements of an activity.

It has to be decided whether this deficiency in current knowledge brings into question the very foundations of a problem that has plagued all governments for 30 years, namely, what should be done to reduce the rise in social security expenditure to a rate compatible with the level of receipts, since the latter cannot be indefinitely increased.

HUNGARIAN EXPERIENCE OF FINANCING SOCIAL SECURITY

The importance and structure of social security benefits

The share of social security benefits in the total income of the population is steadily rising and will continue to rise for some time to come. In the past 10 years, the structure of total income has developed as shown in table 13. Table 14 shows how social security benefits have grown over the same period.

During the period considered the consumer price index rose from 100 to 155. Hence at constant prices the index of social security benefits (1980 as a percentage of 1970) grew as follows:

The highest rates of growth were attained by pensions, family allowances, child-care leave, maternity, social services, and culture, sport and recreation.

At present, social insurance costs represent about 60 per cent of the cost of social security. It should be mentioned that health care is available to Hungarian citizens free of charge; hence its cost is not covered by social insurance.

Financing methods

Since 1945 social security has been financed as follows:
- paid by employers: payroll tax, family allowance contribution, social insurance contribution;
- paid by employees: contribution to pensions scheme;
- receipts from the state budget.

The data in table 15 show the changes in the rates of these contributions from 1945 to 1980.

Until 1979 (except for the period 1953-58), enterprises contributed a payroll tax towards the cost of social security. Organisations financed by the state budget were not subject to this tax, and in some economic sectors certain enterprises were also exempt for reasons of economic policy. In 1980, the payroll tax was abolished in order to reduce production costs.

Table 13.   Hungary: Composition of income, 1970 and 1980

Element of income	Percentage	
	1970	1980
Income from labour	76.1	67.0
Social security benefits	22.6	32.0
Other	1.3	1.0
Total	100.0	100.0

Table 14.   Hungary: Growth of social security benefits, 1970-80

Benefits	Amount (millions of forints, at current prices)		Index (1980 as a percentage of 1970)	
	1970	1980	At current prices	At constant prices
Cash benefits	23 468	87 300	372	240
Pensions	12 985	55 979	431	.
Family allowances	2 810	13 561	483	.
Child-care leave	1 191	3 913	329	.
Sick-pay	4 166	8 534	205	.
Maternity	821	1 895	231	.
Funeral grant	80	98	123	.
Scholarships	491	997	203	.
Other	924	2 323	251	.
Benefits in kind	23 477	60 000	256	165
Health care and medicines	7 313	17 800	243	.
Social services and nurseries	1 111	3 750	338	.
Education, infant school and day-care	9 864	24 800	251	.
Culture, sport, recreation	1 950	7 900	405	.
Other (catering, housing)	3 239	5 750	178	.
Total social security benefits	46 945	147 300	314	202
Including social insurance	21 637	82 990	384	247
As a percentage of total income of the population:				
Cash benefits	11.3	19.0	–	–
Benefits in kind	11.3	13.0	–	–

Table 15. Hungary: Changing rates of social security contributions, 1945-80 (percentage of wages)

Period	Paid by employers			Paid by employees: Contribution to pensions scheme	Total
	Payroll tax	Social insurance contribution	Together		
1945-50	10	20	30	–	30
1951-58	–	10	10	1; 3 (1955)	11; 13
1959-67	15	10	25	3	28
1968-75	8	10; 17	10; 25	3-10 (4 av.)	14; 29
1976-79	13	15; 22	15; 35	3-10 (6 av.)	21; 41
1980	–	10; 13; 17; 24	10-24	3-10 (7 av.)	17-31

From 1946, social insurance contributions amounted to 8 per cent for sickness insurance and 6 per cent for pensions. These contributions, together with the family allowances contribution, amounted to 20 per cent of wages. From 1951 to 1976, apart from some special provisions, sickness insurance and pensions contributions were 6 per cent and 4 per cent of wages respectively, or 10 per cent in all. From 1968 the social insurance contribution was fixed at 17 per cent for employers liable for payroll tax and 10 per cent for the remainder. From 1976 these rates were raised to 22 per cent and 15 per cent respectively. Since 1980, the employers' social insurance contribution has been as follows: 24 per cent for non-agricultural enterprises; 17 per cent for agricultural enterprises; 13 per cent of earnings of members and 17 per cent of wages of employees of agricultural cooperatives; 10 per cent for organisations financed by the state budget; and 24 per cent for other employers.

The differences in contribution rates in the agricultural sector take account of the level of producers' prices and the fact that for co-operative members sickness and maternity benefits are provided not by social insurance but by the co-operatives themselves; accordingly the rate of the social insurance contribution is lower. The 10 per cent rate for organisations financed by the state budget is traditional.

To meet the demands of the labour movement, after 1945 the 3 to 3.5 per cent sickness insurance contribution formerly paid by employees was abolished and the corresponding charge transferred to employers.

In 1951, having regard to the prevailing economic situation and the importance of increasing pensions, the 17th Congress of Trade Unions agreed that from 1952 onwards wage earners should pay a 1 per cent contribution to the pensions scheme. In 1955, the rate was raised to 3 per cent and since 1966 a progressive rate of from 3 to 10 per cent, according to the level of earnings, has been applied.

Table 16. Hungary: Coverage of social security costs, 1976-81

	1976	1977	1980	1981 (estimates)
Social charges (1,000 million forints):				
1. Payroll tax	12.3	13.4	–	–
2. Social insurance contributions paid by–				
Employers	30.6	33.9	43.9	46.0
Employees	10.5	12.1	16.5	18.0
Together	41.1	46.0	60.4	64.0
3. Total social charges (1 + 2)	53.4	59.4	60.4	64.0
Social security benefits (1,000 million forints):				
4. Provided by employers	4.6	4.9	5.7	6.0
5. Social insurance	51.5	56.9	83.0	89.0
6. Provided by the State	36.9	40.9	58.6	64.2
7. Social insurance and state benefits (5 + 6)	88.4	97.8	141.6	153.2
8. Total benefits (4 + 7)	93.0	102.7	147.3	159.2
Proportion of coverage (%):				
Social charges/social insurance and state benefits (3/7)	60.4	60.7	42.7	41.8
Contributions/social insurance benefits (2/5)	79.8	80.8	72.8	71.9
Payroll tax/state benefits (1/6)	33.3	32.8	0.0	0.0
Amount covered by the state budget (1,000 million forints) (7-3)	35.0	38.4	81.2	89.2

In the period 1945-50, the social charges on wages were comparatively high. After reaching their lowest level in the 1950s, they rose again from 1959 onwards. This rising trend only slackened with the abolition of the payroll tax in 1980. However, the payroll tax has been abolished once before only to be restored.

Social charges: role and incidence on wages

Financing of social security

Social security benefits and the wages or income of the population from labour (excluding profit) together constitute the social reproduction value (or cost) of the labour force. If there were no social security benefits an equivalent amount would have to be paid to employees in the form of wages.

Among the various costs of production that enter into the calculation of price, wage costs ought to equal the social reproduction value (or cost) of labour. Consequently, social insurance contributions ought to cover the expenses of social insurance and payroll tax ought to cover the cost of state benefits (apart from benefits provided by employers).

The data in table 16 show that the social charges on wages (tax and contributions) only partially cover the cost of the social benefits provided by social insurance and the State. Partly on account of the abolition of the payroll tax, coverage has declined from about 60 to 40 per cent; the remaining 60 per cent is covered by the state budget out of the proceeds of a tax on profits and other taxes or fiscal receipts.

A rough calculation shows that the social charge on wages would have to be 50 per cent to cover the whole cost of social security. To obtain this 50 per cent, it would be necessary to reintroduce the payroll tax at a rate of 20 per cent instead of the former 13 per cent, and every employer would have to pay this tax at the full rate without rebates or exemptions. The same would apply to social insurance contributions. It appears that social insurance expenditure would be fully covered by contributions if every employer paid contributions at the maximum rate at present in force.

Cost of labour

Social charges on wages (tax and contributions) are part of production costs, and at the level of the national economy they are an element of net national income. Charges on income related to the employment of labour reduce the demand for labour as opposed to that for capital.

If total social charges on wages reach a high enough level to cover the cost of social security benefits, this–together with other elements of production costs–will encourage enterprises to economise on manpower. On the other hand, if they remain below that level, then labour costs will appear to be lower than they really are, which can have a harmful effect on the economical use of labour, encouraging excessive demand and hence causing a manpower shortage.

For many years up to 1980, there was a tax in Hungary of 5 per cent of the value (at first gross value, subsequently net value) of fixed capital assets and stocks. This tax (an artificial cost factor) encouraged enterprises to produce with less capital and more labour, especially since social charges were lower than they should have been. In this way, the relative price levels of capital goods and consumer goods tended to make the use of capital more expensive than that of labour.

These factors helped to maintain full employment, and led eventually to a manpower shortage. It was reasonable to give priority to the use of manpower in the period of extensive development when full employment was the aim. Although that period came to an end years ago, the legislation was not adpated promptly to the changed circumstances.

The tax on assets was abolished in 1980, and the overvaluation of assets and undervaluation of labour were accordingly reduced. Nevertheless, even now there is a considerable gap between the valuation of assets and that of labour. Only a part of the cost of social security appears as a charge on the cost of production.

Level of prices, costs and profits

In the application of social charges on wages, exemptions or lower rates can be, inter alia, a means of maintaining a low level of consumer prices, reducing or equalising costs resulting from certain unfavourable economic conditions, and maintaining a desired level of profit. Such methods constitute indirect subsidies alongside which recourse can be had to direct aid in the form of budget appropriations, subsidies or reimbursement. At present a complicated system of direct and indirect subsidies is applied, whose efficacy and yield are difficult to assess.

In short, it can be said that in present circumstances social charges on wages only partially fulfil their economic function. The rate of the charges (both taxes and contributions) is low, and they do not cover the cost of social security. The cost of wages does not adequately reflect the actual social reproduction value of labour. The legislation makes the use of labour relatively cheap and hence preferable. Finally, tax exemptions and rebates, authorised as a form of indirect subsidy and a means of influencing price levels, make it difficult to assess the efficacy and yield of the system.

Future lines of action

There are not likely to be any radical legislative changes in the short term. Since 1980, a number of significant measures have been adopted in respect of prices and financial policy, but in the present economic situation sweeping reforms do not appear desirable.

In the longer term, a number of measures might be envisaged.

The relative prices of capital goods and of consumer goods should be progressively adjusted, so that capital gradually becomes cheaper and labour more expensive.

The payroll tax should be reintroduced. The global level of charges on wages should be raised sufficiently to cover the cost of benefits provided by social insurance and the State, as well as by employers. In this way wages and social charges together would reflect the actual social reproduction value of the workforce.

The rates of social charges should be the same for all employers without exemptions or rebates. If some employers have to receive special treatment, direct state subsidies should be used in preference to indirect forms of subsidy.

With a fixed rate, the product of social charges on wages is proportionate to the wage bill. Since the cost of social benefits rises more rapidly than wages, the rate of social charges should be raised regularly, every five years or even yearly. It seems advisable to provide for automatic annual adjustment within the framework of long- and medium-term plans, co-ordinated with the planned increases in social security benefits relative to wages. In this way the cost of social benefits would be covered automatically every year.

The cost of social benefits provided by employers should also be accounted as part of wage costs.

Finally, the employee contributions to the pension scheme might be discontinued and an appropriate contribution paid by employers.

These are some of the possible lines of future action. Others could, of course, be suggested. The aim should be the harmonisation of theoretical considerations, practical constraints and traditional practice, and it is this that will no doubt condition future policy.

FINANCING SOCIAL SECURITY IN SPAIN

In analysing the financing of the Spanish social security system four factors have to be borne in mind. The first is the developments that have led to the present situation. The second is the state of Spanish public finances within the context of the present economic crisis, because of its incidence on the system. Next, some consideration must be given to the way in which the social security budget takes account of that situation. And finally, an attempt should be made to foresee the direction in which the financing of the social security system is moving.

Although the Spanish social security system still has the structure it was given by the Act of 28 December 1963, a basic reorganisation is envisaged to take account of a number of factors including the changes in national political conditions (the Constitution of 1978); the new situation in labour relations resulting from the radical reorganisation of trade union forces and employers' groups (Trade Union Association Act of 1 April 1977 and ratification by Spain on 13 April 1977 of the International Agreement on Civil and Political Rights and the International Agreement on Economic, Social and Cultural Rights); and, finally, the severe world economic crisis, which has had very marked repercussions on the Spanish economy.[1]

The question of unemployment insurance, which has remained outside the administrative scope of social security, will not be considered in this paper. Since 1978, unemployment insurance has been largely financed by the State, as well as by contributions from enterprises (3.40 per cent of real earnings) and from employees (0.60 per cent of the same sum). The costs of unemployment benefits are rising very rapidly; they represented 0.02 per cent of gross domestic product in 1960 and 2.6 per cent in 1980, and a deficit of 110,000 million pesetas was forecast for 1981.

The evolution of social security financing

At the outset Spain's social security system was financed in accordance with the funding principle applied by private insurance institutions. This technique gave rise to severe criticism, and the Act of 1963 introduced the pay-as-you-go system of financing; although some traces of funding still survive (in mutual occupational accident funds and for the creation of certain reserves), these are now being rapidly reduced. The capital formerly accumulated was used to sterilise inflationary pressures by subscription to a loan at a very low interest rate to cover the national debt and finance the creation of a number of national enterprises. At present, the social security system has very little capital left and its savings capacity is very low, too low even to cover the investments needed for the operation of its services.

More than four-fifths of social security income is derived from contributions based on wages; two-thirds of this is paid by enterprises. The proportion of social charges in all charges is growing: between 1970 and 1980 the amount of contributions multiplied tenfold whereas that of taxes only increased sixfold. During the same period, the effective rate of contributions rose from 16 to 28 per cent of wages. The cost of manpower rose accordingly.

The three main components of social security expenditure–health care, pensions and unemployment benefits–have increased annually at a rate equivalent to about 1 per cent of GDP. Only in recent years has it been possible to put a brake on this increase in costs.

In the serious situation resulting from the economic crisis, the possibility of maintaining a system financed by a payroll tax is doubtful. Rising labour costs create employment problems, the more serious since the cost of energy is not rising as fast, so that energy is being increasingly substituted for labour. Financing by contributions is a source of great inequalities between sectors and enterprises, and penalises firms that apply the wage policy recommended by the Government. Finally, it weakens competitivity on foreign markets and accentuates present inflationary trends.

Some instruments have, however, been evolved in order to co-ordinate social security financial policy and integrate it more successfully into the economy as a whole. For example, there is now complete uniformity of budgeting and of recording of assets for all schemes, which is itself a valuable instrument for effective economic policy. In addition, a whole range of budgetary control mechanisms has been instituted.

The financial situation

The first point to be made is that credits allocated to the public sector–for central administration, social security, autonomous bodies and public enterprises–have increased substantially from 183,800 million pesetas in

Table 17. Spain: Consumption, capital resources and investment as a percentage of gross national disposable income (GNDI), 1978-80

Item	Percentages of GNDI		
	1978	1979	1980
1. Consumption	78.3	79.6	81.2
2. Capital resources ("savings")	21.7	20.4	18.9
3. Gross investment	20.8	20.3	21.3
4. Balance or external deficit (2-3)	+1.0	+0.1	−2.4

Source: Bank of Spain.

1977 to 1,201,800 million in April 1981; these credits are financed in the main by loans from the Bank of Spain.

In 1980 the final deficit of the public sector was 515,400 million pesetas–3.4 per cent of Gross National Disposable Income (GNDI). This aggravated the situation as regards savings, which had amounted to 25 per cent of GNDI in the period 1970-74 and fell sharply in subsequent years (see table 17).

Expenditure on social activities rose from 59.5 per cent of public sector expenditure in 1969 to 70 per cent in 1980. Present public sector investments in this area may be expected to produce a very sharp increase in current expenditure and, as a result, a new drop in "savings" within the system as a whole.

The Spanish economy is thus faced with a whole series of financing problems, in which the behaviour of the public sector now plays a crucial role. The forecast by the Bank of Spain that the public sector debt will further increase, to reach between 800,000 million and 1 million million pesetas in 1982 is therefore particularly disquieting, the more so since GDP is stagnant (1981 was expected to be a year of zero growth).

In the circumstances, it may be wondered how the social security system can, without losing its effectiveness, change its mode of financing so as not to cause serious harm to the national economic structure.

The social security budget [2]

Under the General Budget Act of 4 January 1977, the Government is required every year to append to the general state budget a summary of the social security budget and a whole series of documents, including a financial and economic report explaining how the estimates of income and expenditure have been established.

This budget does not, however, cover all social security benefits. Under the royal decree of 16 November 1978 it excludes unemployment benefits, benefits paid by various public services (for civil servants), ben-

Table 18.   Spain: Social expenditure in 1980

Item	Expenditure (1,000 million pesetas)
Social benefits provided by public agencies, excluding direct production:	
Social security system:	
Cash	1 127.3
Transfers to families for specific purposes (medicaments, approved hospitalisation, etc.)	295.1
Other social security agencies	42.7
National Employment Institute	310.9
Other public agencies (non-working persons, civil war pensions, national funds, etc.)	288.9
Public expenditure on the direct production of social welfare services:	
Social security system	342.0
Health and social services from the rest of the public sector (estimate)	60.0
Private sector social benefits (estimate)	80.0
Total	2 546.9

efits paid to economically inactive groups and under the head of war pensions, etc. There has been no reorganisation in this area so far, but it is hoped that this work will be done in 1982 by the Health and Social Security Research Institute, which has been charged with the preparation of the Spanish social budget for 1983.

Using various sources, it has been possible to establish the estimate of social expenditure set out in Table 18. The total of this expenditure represents about 17 per cent of GDP (70 per cent of the total is for social security). This is far from being as high a proportion of GDP as that attained by the countries of the European Community, but it is increasing rapidly: at current prices social benefits multiplied tenfold in the period 1971-81 whereas GDP increased only sixfold, and the rise in benefits was faster in the second half of the decade (economic crisis, growing unemployment).

Turning to social security income proper, the 1982 budget shows that 83 per cent is obtained from contributions. Since 1978 contribution income has grown as shown in table 19.

Since, between 1978 and 1982, the growth indices for the two major items of expenditure–cash benefits and health care–have risen from 100 to 199.05 and 159.35 respectively, it appears that contributions–which have the obvious advantage of being easy to collect–can keep pace with the rising cost of health care but not with that of cash benefits.

Table 19.   Spain: Contribution income, 1978-82

Year	Total contribution income (1,000 million pesetas)	Index of growth (1978 = 100)
1978 [1]	1 185.926	100.00
1979 [1]	1 431.777	120.73
1980 [2]	1 540.132	129.87
1981 [2]	1 812.910	152.87
1982 [2]	1 941.413	163.70

[1] Accounts figures.   [2] Budget figures.

The growth of social security expenditure in the strict sense of the term and of each of its major branches in absolute figures and as a percentage of GDP is shown in table 20.

Relative to GDP it appears that social security expenditure has not increased since 1979. Whereas pension payments continued to grow (although more slowly than before), health care expenditure has tended to decline.

Current financing options

The problem to be faced is twofold: the need to meet the social welfare expenses inherent in the social security system and to do so within the framework of efforts to solve national economic problems. Particular stress may have been laid on the second aspect, but it should not be forgotten that the solution to the financial problem must be concordant with that of social security needs in general. To reconcile these two aims is one of the major challenges facing the social security authorities in Spain.[3]

To be sure, there are tendencies in Spain, particularly in the most conservative quarters, favouring a return to the funding system, possibly with a large part played by the private sector.[4] But comparison of the evolution of interest rates and retail price indices shows that a funding system would have virtually insurmountable disadvantages in Spain. A moment's reflection on the brutal drop in stock exchange prices resulting from the economic crisis makes it clear that this problem is not an easy one to solve.

Nevertheless, a pay-as-you-go system based on wages might become an intolerable burden on contributors. Greater recourse to financing from the state budget is therefore envisaged.

On the one hand, in view of the requirements of the 1978 Constitution, minimum benefits will have to be generalised, and will have to be financed by taxation. In view of Spain's present fiscal problems and its growing budget deficit, it has to be asked what new taxes can be levied for the purpose. The "Second red book on social security" proposes that consideration should be given to the possibility of creating taxes on alcohol, tobacco and automobiles (because of their causal relationship with certain risks covered

Table 20. Spain: Social security expenditure, 1972-82

Items	1972		1976[1]		1978		1979		1980		1981[2]		1982[2]	
	1,000 million current pesetas	% of GDP	1,000 million current pesetas	% of GDP	1,000 million current pesetas	% of GDP	1,000 million current pesetas	% of GDP	1,000 million current pesetas	% of GDP	1,000 million current pesetas	% of GDP	1,000 million current pesetas	% of GDP
Pensions	80.5	2.3	274.8	3.8	572.9	5.1	749.0	5.7	919.7	6.1	1 129.3	6.4	1 283.8	6.4
Temporary incapacity for work	16.3	0.5	52.1	0.7	96.4	0.9	121.6	0.9	111.4	0.7	124.9	0.7	132.4	0.7
Provisional disability	4.4	0.1	7.5	0.1	14.6	0.1	20.7	0.1	22.4	0.1	25.7	0.1	26.9	0.1
Family protection	57.1	1.7	59.9	0.8	60.1	0.5	62.6	0.5	54.0	0.4	54.1	0.3	54.1	0.3
Other benefits	6.9	0.2	15.5	0.2	13.7	0.1	12.6	0.1	12.1	0.1	11.5	0.1	11.1	0.1
Total economic benefits	165.2	4.8	409.8	5.6	757.7	6.7	966.5	7.3	1 119.6	7.4	1 345.5	7.6	1 508.3	7.6
Health benefits	81.5	2.4	231.1	3.2	409.4	3.6	457.3	3.5	509.6	3.4	574.2	3.3	654.8	3.2
Social services	2.2	0.1	5.5	0.1	8.2	0.1	10.5	0.1	22.0	0.1	24.2	0.1	29.9	0.1
Overheads and miscellaneous costs	12.7	0.3	31.8	0.4	43.8	0.4	49.7	0.4	68.4	0.4	76.1	0.4	81.8	0.4
Total	261.6	7.6	678.2	9.3	1 219.1	10.8	1 484.2	11.3	1 719.6	11.4	2 020.0	11.4	2 274.8	11.3

1 Because of changes in the accounting system, the figures for 1976 had to be estimated on the basis of the year's accounts. 2 GDP was estimated at 17,560,000 million current pesetas for 1981 and 20,194,000 million for 1982.

by social security); or taxes to finance certain special schemes (such as exist in agriculture and stock-breeding); or a partial attribution of value added tax, the introduction of which is currently before Parliament.

As far as employer and employee contributions are concerned, consideration is being given to increasing the wage ceiling gradually so as to bring contributions closer to what they would be if actual earnings were taken as a base, which would seem likely to lead to a more even distribution of the burden among firms and sectors, while at the same time diminishing the share paid by employers and, of course, increasing that paid by employees.

Currently, social security is keenly debated in Spain. It is especially significant that the major trade unions–the Trade Union Confederation of Workers' Committees linked with the Spanish Communist Party, and the General Workers' Union associated with the Spanish Workers' Socialist Party–readily accept the need for a marked shift in financing towards the general tax system, agreeing in this with the Spanish Confederation of Employers Organisations (any differences of opinion being in the area of administration and other fields). It seems clear that this concordance of views could rapidly lead to a structure of social security financing in Spain quite different from that at present in existence.

FINANCING SOCIAL SECURITY IN THE UNITED STATES

The different social security programmes and methods of financing them

There are a number of different social security programmes in the United States. Some are operated solely by the Federal Government; others are the joint responsibility of the Federal Government and the states; and yet others are under the sole jurisdiction of the states. (It should be noted that in the United States the definition of social security is much narrower than that given by the ILO's Social Security (Minimum Standards) Convention, 1952 (No. 102); it usually covers only the old-age, survivors and disability insurance programme.)

Old-age, survivors and disability insurance (OASDI)

This federally operated programme covers almost all workers in the country (including the self-employed since 1951) and in outlying areas such as Puerto Rico. The only major exceptions are most civilian employees of the Federal Government and some employees of state and local governments. Although railroad workers have a separate system, it is so closely co-ordinated with OASDI, as regards both benefits and financing, that it may be considered that they are really covered by the general system.

Ever since OASDI was established, by legislation passed in 1935 and brought into force in 1937, its financing has been based largely on equal contribution rates for employers and employees (5.35 per cent each in 1981). These are levied on wages and salaries up to a yearly ceiling; this earnings base has varied over the years, beginning with $3,000, from 1937 to 1950, and reaching $29,700 in 1981. As regards self-employed persons, the "compromise" basis of their contribution was fixed at 1.5 times the rate for employees (although a somewhat lower proportion prevailed in 1973-80, this will not be the case in future).

Other sources of financing–relatively quite small–have been interest on trust-fund assets and certain payments from the General Fund of the Treasury of the United States. In 1980, interest receipts represented 1.9 per cent of the total receipts of the OASDI Trust Funds. Payments from the General Fund are made to cover additional benefits paid to former members of the armed forces for non-contributory wage credits granted for service before 1957 (when contributory coverage was instituted) and, for service since 1956, to cover the cost of crediting larger amounts of earnings than were actually paid, as a reflection of payments in kind (the State in effect paying contributions retroactively for this category of persons); they also cover benefits paid to persons who had reached the age of 72 before 1972 and were not insured under OASDI, who receive uniform, flat-rate benefits adjusted from time to time for changes in the price level. The total payments for these two categories in 1980 were only 0.5 per cent of the total receipts of OASDI (0.4 per cent for members of the armed forces and 0.1 per cent for the non-insured over-72 group).

Initially the OASDI programme was financed on a partial-reserve basis, so that a substantial interest-earning fund would be built up, which would meet part of the benefit expenditure over the long run. This would not have resulted in full actuarial reserves such as life insurance companies are required by law to hold, and such as private pension plans aim to accumulate after a period of years. Over the years less and less emphasis was placed on the partial-reserve basis, and for the past decade financing has been on a current-cost or pay-as-you-go basis, with small contingency reserves. Various experts have advocated that the trust-fund balance should be equal to anything from six months' to one year's outgo, but at present it is well below that level with a ratio of about two months' outgo at the end of 1981.

The assets of OASDI have always been invested in obligations of the Federal Government (or obligations guaranteed by it as to principal and interest).

Hospital insurance

This social insurance programme is operated in conjunction with OASDI. It provides hospital care (and certain related benefits) for insured persons and their spouses who are aged 65 or over and to insured persons who have been receiving monthly disability benefits for at least two years. Protected persons pay relatively small cost-sharing amounts.

When hospital insurance was introduced in 1966, the basis for both employer and employee contributions was established in the same way as for OASDI, that is, at equal rates (1.3 per cent each in 1981). The rate for self-employed persons was set at the same level as for employees, and this is still the case today. OASDI and hospital insurance contributions are collected as a unit.

Hospital insurance also receives interest payments on its investments. In 1980, such receipts accounted for only 4.3 per cent of its total income. In addition, certain payments are made to it from the General Fund for members of the armed forces and for persons having reached the age of 65 before 1975, who were not covered but receive hospital insurance benefits. These payments amounted to only 2.8 per cent of total receipts in 1980.

Since its inception, the financing basis for hospital insurance has been more or less on a current-cost basis. The size of the trust fund considered desirable is from six months' to one year's outgo (the level at the end of 1981 being five-and-a-half months).

The assets are invested in the same manner as those of OASDI.

Supplementary medical insurance

This programme is also operated by the Federal Government. Participation is open on a voluntary basis to all persons in the country aged 65 or over and for disabled OASDI beneficiaries who have been receiving benefits for at least two years. About 95 per cent of old persons and 90 per cent of the disabled do in fact choose to be covered. The programme reimburses doctors' fees and certain other related costs. Benefits generally cover about 70-80 per cent of these costs, after the insured persons have paid a relatively small deductible yearly cost-sharing contribution.

When the programme first came into effect in 1966, it was applicable only to persons aged 65 and over. It was financed by uniform monthly contributions from insured persons and matching contributions from the general revenues of the Federal Government. When long-term disabled persons receiving cash benefits under OASDI were brought within the scope of supplementary medical insurance in 1972, their contribution was set at the same rate as that of the aged, although their cost per head was higher; as a result, the corresponding government contribution was higher and no longer equal.

In 1975, the matching principle was abandoned for the aged as well, and the government contribution was raised to over 50 per cent, since the contributions from insured persons can no longer rise more rapidly than OASDI benefits, which are adjusted for changes in the price level.

At present, contributions for aged insured persons cover only 24 per cent of their costs, while those for disabled persons cover only 15 per cent.

The programme is also financed by interest payments on its investments, which in 1980 amounted to 3.8 per cent of total receipts. Supplementary medical insurance is considered to be a short-term rather than a long-term programme, because the contributions from insured persons plus the matching contribution from the General Fund of the Treasury are intended to equal, each year, the cost of the benefits and related administrative expenses. As a result, if experience follows the estimates, the balance available at any time (especially at the end of each contribution year) should be at least as large as the incurred claims for benefits outstanding. This financing standard is the same as that applicable by private health insurance companies.

The assets of the programme are invested in the same manner as those of OASDI and hospital insurance.

Unemployment insurance

All the states, in co-operation with the Federal Government, have established social insurance programmes to provide unemployment benefits. These cover about the same workers as OASDI (except self-employed workers). A separate nationwide programme, administered by the Federal Government, is provided for railroad workers. Benefits are earnings-related and are payable for a maximum of 39 weeks.

These programmes are financed solely by a contribution from employers (except for a small employee contribution in three states). The contribution rate is applicable generally only to the first $6,000 of annual earnings. It varies among employers and in different years depending on the unemployment benefit experience of each enterprise. In general the contribution rate has varied between 2 and 3.5 per cent in recent years, although it has been much lower for some employers and somewhat higher for others.

The only payments from the General Fund of the Treasury into the unemployment insurance trust fund, which is held by the Federal Government, are with respect to the unemployment benefits paid to federal employees and interest on the investments of the trust fund. In addition, if the trust fund has insufficient funds to meet benefit expenditures, it can obtain interest-free loans from the General Fund (constituting a form of government subsidy). The total of such loans as of August 1981 amounted to $14,000 million.

Because of the cyclical nature of unemployment, the unemployment insurance programme is naturally financed on a contingency-reserve basis. The balances tend to build up in times of good economic conditions and vice versa. The assets of the unemployment insurance trust fund, like those of the other programmes, are invested in federal government securities.

Temporary disability insurance

Five states and Puerto Rico have established temporary disability programmes. A separate, nationwide programme, administered by the Federal Government, is provided for railroad workers. The workers covered are generally the same as those covered by unemployment insurance. The benefits are earnings-related and are usually payable for up to 26 weeks, after which disability benefits may be payable under OASDI.

The various programmes are financed by contributions based on wages up to a specified ceiling. In two programmes only employees contribute; the reason for this is that in these instances there had originally been an employee tax for unemployment insurance, but this was eliminated and used for the temporary disability insurance programme when it was introduced. Financing is shared equally (or about equally), in four programmes, while in the railroad workers' programme it is borne entirely by the employers.

Since these programmes (other than the railroad programme) are the sole responsibility of the states, no payments are made to them from the General Fund of the Treasury (except for interest on the investments of the railroad programme).

Financing is on the basis of contingency reserves. The assets are invested in various ways but, except in the case of the railroad programme, not generally in obligations of the Federal Government.

Workmen's compensation

All states have workmen's compensation programmes. In a few, these programmes are administered solely by the state. In the remainder, insurance companies provide the legally required benefits. The Federal Government has established a separate programme for its own employees (and also a nationwide programme for longshoremen and harbour workers in the private sector). Both cash benefits for disabled workers and survivors of deceased workers and medical care for disabled workers are provided by these programmes.

These programmes are financed by contributions based on total payroll, the rates varying with the nature of the industry and the experience of the particular employer. In all state programmes the employer bears the whole cost, which averages slightly less than 2 per cent of total payroll for the entire country. No payments are made by the Federal Government (except, of course, in its capacity as employer).

Generally speaking, the various workmen's compensation programmes are financed on a mixed basis. The various insurance carriers (both state funds and commercial insurance companies) finance short-term benefits (temporary disability cash and medical care benefits) on the basis of contingency reserves. The long-term benefits (permanent disability and survivors' cash benefits) are usually financed on a fully-funded basis by setting up the full actuarial reserves when claims are awarded. The assets are invested in various ways, but not generally in obligations of the Federal Government.

* * *

In addition to the insurance programmes discussed above, some welfare programmes are financed from general revenue (without the creation of reserves).

The problem of adapting financing methods

From an economic standpoint the matter of who pays the contributions or taxes necessary to finance a social security programme is not important. It can be argued endlessly whether employer contributions are actually borne by the employees in the form of lower wages, or by the general public (which consists primarily of workers and their families) in the form of higher prices. In any event, it is very unlikely, in an economic sense, that employers pay their contributions entirely (or even largely) from their own resources, without integrating them as production costs into the general price structure of their products. In the same manner, it is usually assumed that the workers' contributions, if any, are paid entirely by the workers.

But it can be argued that, in collective bargaining, the workers are essentially concerned with the "bottom line" of their take-home pay, that is, its net value. If so, the workers' contribution is merely one of the many "costs of production" and is passed on to consumers (again predominantly workers) in the long run through the price structure.

In the view of the author of the study summarised here old-age, survivors and disability insurance and hospital insurance should continue to be financed solely by earnings-based contributions–and not from general revenue, whether in the form of specially earmarked taxes or not. (The small portion of the income of the respective trust funds that comes from the General Fund of the Treasury does not involve general financing on a permanent basis; it serves either for special limited groups of persons or as the matching employer contribution with respect to covered employees of the Federal Government.) This method of financing is desirable in order to make the cost of the programmes apparent to the general public. The injection of general revenues might lead uninformed people to believe that "somebody else" is paying for their benefits, thus generating demands for ever-larger benefits.

It is often argued that the earnings-based contributions to OASDI and hospital insurance are regressive and bear too heavily on low-income workers, whereas other taxes that might be used to finance these programmes are more progressive. In fact, when both contributions and benefits are considered as a whole, the combination is not regressive since the contributions are proportional to earnings up to a ceiling, benefits are heavily weighted in favour of the lower earners and the benefits and contributions are the same for all workers at or above the earnings ceiling.

Perhaps even more important, the incidence of taxes cannot really be measured accurately. Any change in the tax structure will, after a short time, be accompanied by a readjustment of the incomes and remuneration structure. Placing a new tax on employers will shortly result in a readjustment of the price and wage structure. Similarly, an increase in the income tax rate for those with higher earnings will result in a change in the structure of salaries and fringe benefits and of the fees of self-employed persons.

Thus, the financing of OASDI and hospital insurance in any other way than by earnings-related contributions would actually result in a shifting of taxes, so that it cannot be said with assurance whether the actual incidence of the taxes would be significantly different from the impact of increased contributions. It cannot be determined who now really pays the employer contributions. Some argue that they are borne by the workers through lower wages, while others claim that they are covered by higher prices, which in turn are paid in large part by the covered workers. In fact, there is no way of measuring this factor precisely—or even coming close to doing so.

If new taxes were not levied to meet the cost of any general revenues injected into the OASDI and hospital insurance programmes, this would eventually add to the budget deficit and increase inflation, so that people would be paying for the government subsidy in any case. Direct and visible contributions are a better, more honest way of financing these programmes.

At times it is contended, in support of general-revenue financing for OASDI and hospital insurance that the "social cost" of a social security programme—if it is to be truly social—might appropriately be paid for, at least in part, by society as a whole. Under a system that covers virtually all workers in the country there is little difference between "society as a whole" and the covered workers and employers. Accordingly, why abandon the visible, forthright system of earnings-based contributions for the obscure system of general-revenue or budget-deficit financing?

The same proposition is sometimes supported by pointing out that the supplementary medical insurance programme is financed to a significant extent (roughly 70 per cent) by payments from general revenue. However, this is not a social insurance programme but rather subsidised voluntary insurance. As such, it is only natural and proper that there should be financing from a source other than the insured persons; such other source can logically only be the General Fund of the Treasury.

Notes

[1] See Instituto de Estudios de Sanidad y Seguridad Social (IESSS): *Informe sobre el estado actual del sistema español de la seguridad social* (Madrid, 1976) ("Red book on social security"); idem: *Criterios para la racionalización y mejora de la seguridad social* (Madrid, 1981) and *Propuesta de medidas de racionalización y mejora de la seguridad social española* (Madrid, 1981) (these two publications are known together as the "Second red book on social security").

[2] See Ministerio de Trabajo, Sanidad y Seguridad Social: *Proyecto de presupuesto del sistema de seguridad social 1982* (Madrid, 1981).

[3] A. Durán Heras: "La financiación de los gastos de salud", and C. Monasterio: "La reforma de la financiación de la seguridad social española", in *Información comercial española* (Madrid), July-Aug. 1981, pp. 151-158 and 163-167.

[4] "Dossier seguridad social", in *Horizonte empresarial* (Barcelona), Sep. 1981, pp. 16-37, and S. Arancibia: "Fondo de pensiones: la privatización en marcha", in *Perspectivas y mercado* (Madrid), Oct. 1981, pp. 59-62.

PART THREE

FUTURE PERSPECTIVES

RATIONALISATION OF SOCIAL SECURITY FINANCING

5

Guy Perrin *

A basic aspect of the general reform of social security relates to its financial organisation. It warrants special interest at present since the periodic problem due to recurrent financial difficulties besetting social security has now become acute in the highly developed systems while the savings that may be expected from institutional, administrative or technical rationalisation projects will probably not suffice to prevent a general review of traditional methods of financing. Such a review cannot be avoided in any case because of the increased costs resulting from trends towards the universal application and harmonisation of social security, accentuating the maladjustment of the financial model of social insurance, especially for the protection of non-active persons.

Such a review would gain in value, however, if it were approached not only from the utilitarian standpoint of adjusting resources to expenditure but also from the standpoint of financial rationalisation, so as to try to improve the logical conformity of financing methods to the essential functions of social security, to the responsibilities incumbent on the insured persons, enterprises and the State, and to the country's economic capacity. In this connection, the concern for efficiency in making social security charges should not be dissociated from an appraisal of the methods used, of the clarity, equity and compatibility with the need for economic equilibrium. If social security deductions are better understood, more broadly accepted and reasonably adapted to the economic environment, they will doubtless prove more productive. In this sense, the method of making deductions is more significant than the amount deducted.

Hence there is a need at present to work out a new financial approach that will take into account the technical, social and economic conditions on which the possibility of adapting means to growing needs for social protection depends, and this with a threefold view to a selective appropriation of resources, the equitable apportionment of costs and the most satisfactory

---

* International Labour Office.

relationship between methods of financing and the objectives of economic policy.

SELECTIVE APPROPRIATION OF RESOURCES

First of all, a selective appropriation of resources would bring greater clarity to a field where the development of social security systems has often led to a systematic increase in contributions, especially for employers, and to makeshift arrangements rather than well-thought-out research and innovation. When social insurance schemes were first being introduced, however, the use of the different sources of funds was governed by simple logic, of an institutional nature. In the course of time, this gave way, especially under the influence of the administrative unification of social security, to a new, functional organisation of financing.

The institutional approach

At the outset the methods of financing were largely determined by the type of protection provided. While social assistance resorted traditionally to public funds, social insurance was financed by the contributions of workers and employers, except for employment injury coverage, which was financed solely by employers' contributions, contribution by workers always being exceptional,[1] and from the first family allowance schemes financed either from public funds, as in New Zealand in 1926, or more often by employers' contributions alone, as in Australia (New South Wales) in 1927, in Belgium in 1930 and in France in 1932. The latter system made it possible to achieve nationwide compensation of the cost of wage supplements granted by certain employers and certain public administrations to cover the family expenses met by their workers. The State intervened only secondarily, especially in pensions insurance. The first German old-age and invalidity insurance scheme introduced by the Act of 22 June 1889 provided for a state contribution of 50 marks per insured person annually, owing to the need for a solidarity contribution to offset the insufficient contributing capacity of insured persons whose incomes were modest by definition, since the membership ceiling was fixed at 2,000 marks per year.[2] Similarly, the French Act of 5 April 1910 concerning workers' and peasants' retirement provided for a pension corresponding to the life capitalisation of paid-up contributions and a life annuity payable by the State, which originally was fixed at 60 francs and, in 1912, increased to 100 francs a year.[3] Lastly, the British Act of 16 December 1911 extended the tripartite formula of financing to sickness insurance and unemployment insurance. For sickness insurance, besides workers' and employers' contributions collected by means of stamps on the insurance card, the State covered a specific proportion of expenses. For unemployment insurance, workers and employers contributed in the same way at the rate of three-eighths of the expenses each, with the State covering the remaining two-eighths.

In each case, the institutional approach was a logical extension of the type of solidarity underlying the two main forms of protection. On the one hand, social assistance implied general redistributive solidarity since the body of persons receiving assistance was limited only by their state of need or level of resources and not by membership of a trade. On the other, social insurance implied commutative solidarity limited, within the working community, to wage earners. The occupational nature of this solidarity was corroborated in most branches by the double worker-employer contribution, so long as the employer's contribution was supposed to represent a deferred wage. The possible intervention of public funds in the field of social insurance was still no more than a subsidiary guarantee of security intended to ensure that this new scheme of protection would be a stable and permanent one.

The original logic was, however, lost sight of with the introduction of social security which, combining the previous types of protection, assistance as well as insurance, united the traditional methods of financing, regarded as supplementary means of collecting the necessary resources for the operation of the system, in a global approach. In addition, the principle of administrative unification underpinning the modern doctrine of social security entailed at times–although less frequently–the adoption of integrated financing systems breaking the previous links between the types of protection and the corresponding methods of financing.[4] Lastly, the general extension of social security encouraged the establishment of mixed schemes in which the various sources of financing intermingled and merged. In reality the three traditional sources, consisting of workers' contributions, employers' contributions and state participation, continue to be the main sources of social security funds. But their respective shares have evolved because, in order to meet growing needs, it has proved necessary to strike a better balance between them, although it is not always possible to assess their economic effects with accuracy. Systems of financing where there is a marked predominance of one source of funds–public funds in Australia, Denmark or New Zealand, employers' contributions in France, Italy, Portugal, Spain and Sweden–appear to be the most vulnerable in the face of rising expenditure. Furthermore, as a result of the extension of social security to new categories of insured persons, the methods of drawing on these sources have been diversified: in some cases, individual contributions based on occupational earnings have been replaced by contributions levied on every type of income earned by the insured persons [5] or by additional income tax contributions payable by individuals or corporate bodies; in others, government subsidies are granted to social security institutions to ensure their financial equilibrium, or a specific share of their administrative expenses is paid out of public funds; and in still others, revenue from taxes on goods or services is transferred to them. The efforts to renew sources of financing have been greatest, out of necessity, in sickness insurance, particularly by drawing on revenue from taxes on alcohol, tobacco, petrol or car insurance premiums.[6] However, except for the specific case of special schemes for agricultural workers, for which public finance from taxes on produce is a widespread form of levy, usually regarded as occupational, these are marginal innovations whose financial results are still limited, while the more systematic use of the value added tax is still largely the subject of theoretical debate.[7] The few experiments of this kind carried out in Argentina, Belgium and Italy are still too limited or too recent to be conclusive.

The functional approach

Such a development was hardly favourable to selective appropriation of resources, which financial difficulties in the field of social security have made an urgent need again. Certain converging trends reflect financial restructuring tending to promote specialisation in the use of different sources of funds in accordance with the functional conception of social security, which affords useful selection criteria in this respect. These trends are clearer when they are related to the main sectors of social security.

The use of public funds tends to be concentrated in the sectors of health care and compensatory income, in relation either to family allowances or to a guaranteed minimum social income.

In the sector of health care, the use of public funds goes hand in hand with the establishment of nationwide public health services. However, national insurance schemes–owing to their historical origins in the generalisation of previous sickness insurance schemes–continue to be financed by a double contribution from insured persons and employers. Public funds, from state or local community sources, are nevertheless normally added to this double contribution.

In the sector of guaranteed social income support, a similar trend is found in the financing of family allowances and the minimum social income. As regards family allowances, the switchover of most universal schemes to financing out of public funds is particularly significant. This is the case in particular in Australia, Canada, the German Democratic Republic, the Federal Republic of Germany, Ireland, New Zealand, the Scandinavian countries, the United Kingdom and the USSR. This switchover shows that the financing of family allowance schemes by employers' contributions (due to the historical circumstances in which the schemes were originally established), loses its initial justification when the schemes are extended to the entire population. France and the Netherlands are among the rare countries where these benefits have been extended to the whole population, on 1 January 1978 and 1980 respectively, with contributions from employers and the self-employed alone. In France, however, the financing of the scheme from tax revenue is under official consideration. In addition it has already been decided to transfer the cost of compensation for handicapped adults to the state budget. In Austria and Israel, which also have universal family allowance schemes, both methods of financing, from public funds and by means of employer contributions, are used in parallel. However, in some countries where family allowances are universal, such as Belgium, Finland and Luxembourg, state participation is more selective, being limited to financing certain benefits only: benefits subject to a means test in Belgium, birth grants in Finland, and birth grants, prenatal, postnatal and maternity allowances, increased family allowances having regard to age, and supplementary allowances for disabled persons in Luxembourg, plus any deficit. Even in countries where family allowance schemes are limited to workers only, state participation in their financing, in one form or another, tends to develop, not only as a means of ensuring financial equilibrium but as a structural component designed to give solidarity a national dimension in the provision of family allowances. This is the case in particular in Bolivia, Bulgaria, Chad, the Congo, Costa Rica, Czechoslovakia, Finland, Hungary, Italy, the Ivory Coast, Japan, Mali, the Niger, Senegal, Spain, Switzerland (in the scheme for agricultural workers and small farmers) and Tunisia. In Yugoslavia, however, the State intervenes only for the benefit of agricultural workers in a particularly underprivileged autonomous region. The participation of the workers themselves, in addition to employers' contributions, is required in exceptional cases in Greece, Spain and Yugoslavia where the family allowance schemes are assimilated to social insurance schemes. The use of public funds to guarantee a minimum social income reflects the traditional practice of social assistance, which is gradually being taken over by social security. This is confirmed by research in hand which envisages the financing of basic social or family income by the new social taxation system, the practical application of which is now under study in various countries.

On the other hand, guaranteed replacement income continues to be financed largely by contributions from employers and employees. Such income is intended to replace, temporarily or permanently, all or part of earned income in certain specified circumstances,[8] with the possible aid of government subsidies, particularly for pensions insurance. Moreover, these contributions are technically well adapted to the type of protection provided in the form of cash benefits, the amount of which is linked to that of the wages subject to contributions. In this respect, financing by contributions has the advantage of establishing a direct link between receipts and expenditure, not only for the initial benefits but also for their subsequent adaptation to wage trends. However, the financing of different schemes of protection against occupational hazards continues largely to follow traditional practice and draw exclusively on employers' contributions, with a few specific exceptions. The direct participation of workers in the financing of employment injury schemes exists only in Afghanistan and a few states of the United States. Likewise, state participation in such schemes is extremely rare, with the exception of Cuba where financing is entirely public, as well as Chad and Egypt, where the State shares with the employer the financing of the scheme. Lastly, the new sector of employment retraining programmes and social advancement, under the influence of related unemployment insurance and assistance schemes, makes joint use of two sources of funds, employer/employee contributions and public funds.

The road to financial rationalisation in a selective appropriation of resources is thus mapped out by reference to the formal conception of the main social security sectors, with the use of institutional criteria that establish a logical link between the functions of protection, the extension of solidarity and the most appropriate methods of financing.

In unified financing systems, the question of the appropriation of resources does not arise in the same terms. In most cases financial unification is only partial, covering primarily the branches of social insurance concerned with guaranteeing a replacement income—including the event of unemployment—as in Cyprus, Norway and the United Kingdom. In systems of this type, financing is normally based on the contributions of the protected persons and employers, plus a participation by the government which, as a general rule, also covers medical care costs, at least in part, non-contributory benefits and family allowances. The search for a selective appropriation of resources is feasible in partially unified financing systems, but as financial unification advances, its usefulness is reduced to ensuring adequate distribution of sources of funds. A golden rule has even been formulated and applied in the United Kingdom, according to which the optimum distribution of resources is one-third each from employers, workers and public funds. Finally, it has no further justification in a completely unified system, as in Malta, except as regards the residual part of social assistance, traditionally financed out of public funds, and even less in financing systems unified mainly on the basis of public funds, such as those in Australia, Denmark and New Zealand. The same distinction applies for the countries of Eastern Europe. When their financing system is only partially unified, as in the German Democratic Republic, Hungary, Romania and the USSR, the question of a selective appropriation of resources still retains some significance. In these countries, the branches belonging to the unified system are financed wholly by the contributions of workers (except in the USSR), the contributions of enterprises and a variable participation of the public authorities, while the State covers primarily the branches falling outside the unified system, namely medical care (except in the German Democratic Republic) and family benefits (except in Hungary). On the other hand, this question presents less interest in Albania, Bulgaria, Czechoslovakia and Poland, where the financing system is completely unified, except for medical care which is covered entirely by the State.

EQUITABLE APPORTIONMENT OF COSTS

Besides the selective appropriation of resources, which aims at a rational use of financing sources based on institutional or functional criteria, financial rationalisation should also be designed to meet a concern for equity in the apportionment of social security costs among the contributing parties, arising from a need for social rationality. The criteria for evaluating financial equity may relate either to the attribution of specific liabilities to protected persons, employers or the State [9] or to the adaptation of social security levies to the contributing capacity of the liable persons and enterprises.

Development of the sharing of financial liabilities

In the classical financing model, the sharing of financial liabilities was closely linked to the historical development of the various branches, resulting in the equal sharing of social insurance [10] contributions between workers and employers, the preponderant or exclusive role of employers in respect of protection against occupational hazards or compensation for family dependants, and the intervention of public funds for the social categories or hazards not covered by schemes related to employment but pertaining to national solidarity. Protection in the event of unemployment was the joint liability of employers and workers in the case of unemployment insurance schemes, the liability of the community in the case of unemployment assistance schemes, or the liability of the parties involved in financing these two types of schemes.

Here too, with the transition to the modern doctrine of social security, the development of financing methods altered the traditional balance in the apportionment of costs. First of all, the formula of equal sharing between workers and employers [11] in the branches financed by the combined contributions of workers and employers gradually disappeared under the influence of a new approach to liability for protection, tending to lighten the contributions payable by workers [12] and to counterbalance this by increasing employers' contributions or the participation of the public authorities. Employers pay higher contributions than workers in Belgium, France, Italy, Norway, Spain, Sweden and the United Kingdom, in particular. Favouring a radical application of this approach, certain countries in Eastern Europe, such as Albania, Bulgaria, Czechoslovakia, Poland, Romania (except for voluntary pensions insurance) and the USSR, as well as Cuba and Viet Nam, have systematically done away with all workers' contributions. Iceland has adopted a similar approach, except for sickness insurance, as has Sweden where the formula was recently extended to all branches of social insurance, except unemployment insurance. Italy, for its part, has maintained workers' contributions only for pensions insurance.

At the same time, the incorporation of techniques taken from social assistance into swiftly expanding non-contributory schemes, especially for

127

economically non-active persons, led to an increase in the share of public funds in social security financing, although without reducing the relative weight of social assistance schemes, while certain countries deliberately earmarked funds from the government budget for the total or partial financing of measures involving national responsibility: in Belgium, these measures include, under the Act of 29 June 1981 establishing the general principles of social security for wage earners, medical care for pensioners, invalidity, old-age and survivors' benefits and compensation for pneumoconiosis; in Finland, basic survivors' protection and birth grants; in France, additional allowances from the National Solidarity Fund since 1 January 1979 and care for patients hospitalised for more than three years, under the economic recovery measures adopted on 25 July 1979; in Luxembourg, care for particularly costly diseases, the fixed share of pensions and likewise allowances from the National Solidarity Fund, as well as all family benefits other than family allowances proper; and in Switzerland, invalidity benefits for which the contributions of the public authorities–which are general in the field of pensions insurance–amount to half the cost (three-quarters for the account of the Confederation and one-quarter for the account of the cantons). Similarly, the universal application of entitlement to family allowances has most often involved a corresponding appropriation from the government budget, except in a few countries, such as Austria, Belgium, Finland, France, Israel, Luxembourg and the Netherlands, whose schemes are financed, at least in part, by contributions.

Lastly, even the financial structure of employment injury schemes has in some cases been affected by the modern conception of social security, on account of their inclusion in a wholly or partly unified financial system drawing on the contributions of the workers themselves,[13] the establishment of a scheme for protection against incapacity for work where individual contributions are added to the employer's contributions, as in the Netherlands; the co-ordination with the sickness compensation scheme, as in Denmark and Norway, or with the medical care scheme, as in Sweden; or the provision by a publicly financed national service of medical care to workers who have sustained an employment injury or are suffering from an occupational disease, as in most Eastern European countries, as well as Denmark and the United Kingdom. However, with a very few exceptions, employment injury schemes generally follow more closely their traditional financial model, based on the sole liability of employers. This model has been easily integrated in the general conception of social security financing in the countries of Eastern Europe, with the exception of the German Democratic Republic and Hungary. It has even been followed in New Zealand and Switzerland, in the extension of protection against accidents of all kinds as applied to employment injuries to workers. Compensation for non-employment injuries, on the other hand, is financed by a special tax on motor vehicles in the case of traffic accidents and, in the case of other injuries to economically non-active persons, by state participation in medical care expenses in New Zealand, and by the insured persons' individual contributions in Switzerland.

The developments described above show that the traditional model for the apportionment of costs has been abandoned primarily because of the extension of coverage and scope of social security, which has resulted not only in increased financial requirements but also in an enlargement and diversification of participation in the costs of protection. At the present stage, at all events, the financial rationalisation needed for greater equity requires a new approach to the sharing of these costs. The notion of sharing is, however, controversial, since the financing methods usually associated with it are often misleading, except for individual contributions whose burden is borne directly by the designated person owing them. For one thing, the contributions of employers–it would be more accurate to say of enterprises–are a convenient way of passing on social security charges to the labour cost included in the price of goods and services. The success of this formula, used in various fields of labour law, shows that it is a fairly easy way of charging to enterprises the administrative cost of collecting contributions, while remaining vague about who ultimately bears their economic cost. However, neither the notion of deferred wages nor that of social costs, which express two aspects of the same reality, settles the question of the actual attribution of the financial liability behind that reality. Only an economic analysis can shed some light on this issue, although it is often a light full of contrasts if account is taken of the conflicting views that the enterprise contributions are ultimately borne entirely by the workers through a limitation on wage rises,[14] or that they are borne by the employers, the shareholders or the consumers.[15]

Assuming that there is no single, definite answer to the question of the ultimate incidence of enterprise contributions, it is essential to reach agreement at least on their objective basis, which is independent of their legal definition. Such agreement, able to still old debates and put an end to false quarrels, is a prerequisite for the rationalisation of social security financing. If entitlement to benefits and the basis of the parties' participation in the administration of social security are dissociated from the choice of the most appropriate methods of financing, enterprise contributions can be appraised in relation to their real purpose, which is the efficient provision of part of the necessary resources for the system by means of a special levy on wages; this can be equated to a tax on labour, the actual amount of which will vary according to the economic and social conditions. It then becomes possible to determine their part appropriate to enterprise contributions in relation to other sources of funds and possibly even to make their share proportional to the economic possibilities of the branch in question. In some countries of Eastern Europe, enterprise contributions are differentiated according to the occupational branch. Collection can also be simplified by applying the rate directly to the total payroll without making allowance for any ceiling. Such rationalised collection of enterprise contributions, which corresponds to the practice existing in several countries that no longer limit earnings liable to contributions in certain branches, at least for wage earners, or even generally (for example, Italy, Norway, Portugal, Sweden and most of the countries in Eastern Europe) has also been studied in Belgium [16] and in the United States in connection with proposals for reforming social security financing.

On the other hand, financing social security by means of taxes is not an absolute guarantee of equity. The equity of the social security system, from the financial standpoint, depends on the choice of the tax receipts assigned to it or, if financing comes from undifferentiated public funds, on the equity of the tax system itself. In this connection, it is worth recalling the view prevailing in Denmark, where virtually all social expenditure is financed out of public funds, that the basic advantage of such a system of financing is precisely its equity, given the respective weight of direct and indirect taxation in the country, whereas any possible disadvantages would be political rather than economic. The argument is that while the pressure of taxes is greater and is more keenly felt, as there is a predominant proportion of direct taxes, the economic effects of taxation are spread out more broadly by the budget machinery than those of financing based primarily on enterprise contributions.

At all events, the search for equity can be carried further in those systems, which outnumber the others, where financing is diversified according to the various branches of social security. A sound theory of financial liability in the main social security branches would advocate an apportionment of costs confirming the trend noted in the selective appropriation of resources, in connection with developments making for a new distribution of financing sources, while at the same time identifying that trend in terms more favourable to social equity.

For example, the health sector, in the modern sense of a national scheme for the prevention and treatment of diseases, is the twofold responsibility of the public authorities and the persons protected. It therefore warrants the joint input of public funds and individual contributions,[17] possibly progressive, based on the total income of the individuals making up the nation and taking into account national solidarity of a redistributive nature, which is manifestly desirable in this sector, where hazards are greater for the most underprivileged population groups, owing to the differential social morbidity rates. The share of financing from public funds, for the account of the State and local communities, could include taxes on alcohol, tobacco, motor vehicles and economic activities causing pollution detrimental to public health. An interesting example of the theory of financial liability in action is the Japanese Act of 5 October 1973 which created a scheme for the compensation of damage caused by air and water pollution, which is financed by the responsible industries and, in part, by a tax on motor vehicles. However, apart from the case of undertakings constituting a danger for the environment, the financial liability of employers should logically be limited only to the prevention of occupational hazards and the provision of occupational medicine.

The contribution of protected persons to health care schemes is based on the notion of personal responsibility for health. While the classical sickness insurance schemes often excluded from their coverage activities involving acceptance of increased risks, social security tends rather to influence, through the financing of health protection, behaviour, conduct and activities involving a manifest risk of disease or accident. After the example of France, Belgium has moved in this direction since the adoption of the Act of 23 December 1974 to establish an additional automobile insurance premium for the benefit of the medical care scheme. In addition, under an Act of 21 December 1977, amended on 5 August 1978, a levy on the revenue from excise duties and the value added tax on manufactured tobacco was created for the same purpose. In Switzerland, where so-called "reckless" risks are excluded, compulsory accident insurance for motorcyclists, managed by private companies, has been introduced to replace the public non-employment accident insurance scheme. Seen against the background of the traditional notion of private insurance, a more serious trend emerging at present, under the influence of strict standards of social ethics, is the tendency to sanction the liability ascribed to protected persons, in the event of sickness or invalidity, for their poor state of health by withdrawing their entitlement to benefits. The danger of retrogression created by the difficulties facing social security makes the study of its financing all the more necessary.

As for the guaranteed social replacement income, this continues to be based on the joint liability of employers and workers, since occupational solidarity is thereby created for the benefit of the workers as such, without prejudice to the exemption traditionally and rightly granted them, in respect of protection against occupational hazards. It is generally recognised that the financial liability for a social compensatory income falls to the State and local communities involving as it does solidarity of a redistributive nature. Achieved from the first by public assistance,[18] this solidarity tends today to become a nationwide commitment and to use a combination of new fiscal and social techniques.

Lastly, the sector of employment retraining and social advancement is, like that of medical care, a joint responsibility which should be shared by employers and the State since it involves both occupational solidarity and national solidarity.[19] On the other hand, the financial participation of workers in funding this sector is an unjust legacy of former unemployment protection schemes,[20] since workers cannot be held liable for economic hazards, any more than they are for occupational hazards. In the United States, for example, there are very few states where workers have to contribute to the unemployment insurance scheme, which is normally financed by the contributions of enterprises and federal subsidies. A differentiation of this kind is applied in some of the states of the United States and in the

Netherlands. It is worth recalling in this connection the historical influence of the Unemployment Insurance Bill submitted to the Wisconsin legislature in 1921. Under that Bill, unemployment compensation, based on work-men's compensation, was to be financed solely by employers by means of contributions differentiated according to the specific hazards existing in each branch of industry, so as to encourage preventive efforts by the employers' associations concerned. Likewise, in Italy unemployment insurance is financed solely by employers, with state participation in the administrative expenses. Lastly, the financing of the unemployment insurance scheme in Luxembourg was reorganised under the Act of 30 June 1976 and is now based on contributions by enterprises and public funds (especially the allocation of a proportion of revenue from income tax and local taxes), exclusive of any contributions by workers.

Adapting contributions to capacity to pay

A second criterion of equity has to do with the adaptation of contri-butions to the capacity to pay of the covered persons and enterprises. In financing systems where contributions are based on employment earnings, the main difficulty arises from the still widespread practice of setting a ceil-ing on the income liable to contributions.[21] At the outset, this practice was linked to the delimitation of the personal scope of social insurance legis-lation by means of a membership ceiling. When the membership ceiling was done away with, a contribution ceiling was maintained for the determi-nation of income serving as an assessment basis for contributions and ben-efits, because of theoretical considerations about the purpose of social in-surance and practical concern to limit competition between social charges and public taxes. A ceiling on income liable to contributions, however, results in lightening the relative share of the costs borne by people whose earnings exceed the ceiling, so that in practice they benefit from a decreas-ing scale of contributions. The same holds true for uniform contribution systems which, in reality, have lost much of their importance. Such a decreasing scale of contributions seems particularly unfair as regards ben-efits in kind, where the limitation of income liable to contributions has no bearing on the amount of the benefits the insured persons may be entitled to enjoy and where the most frequent use of the medical care system is made by privileged groups. On the other hand, in the case of cash benefits whose amount is linked to employment earnings prior to the contingency, such a scale is still often regarded as being consistent with the principle of equivalence so dear to insurance, in that the ceiling is taken into account for assessing both benefits and contributions. The ratio of contributions to employment earnings has, however, been re-established under some schemes by doing away with the ceiling. This is the case at least of schemes for wage earners, as in Belgium, in France as regards personal contributions for sickness insurance and widows' and widowers' insurance, as well as gen-erally in Italy, Portugal and the countries of Eastern Europe, except the German Democratic Republic. Other schemes, such as the social insurance scheme in Ecuador and the Italian and Swiss pensions schemes, have even introduced an element of redistributive solidarity by maintaining a ceiling only for the assessment of benefits. Apart from the cases of Hungary and Singapore, however, where the rate or the amount of workers' contributions rises with the wage level, a graduated contribution scale has not yet been established in social security, except through taxation, and then only with prudent moderation. Contributions based on income of all kinds and collected by the general tax authorities are often limited to an income ceiling or fixed as a percentage of assessable income.[22] However, the case of Luxembourg, as regards the financing of the new unemployment insurance scheme, is a noteworthy exception. In France the rising cost of unemployment protection made it necessary in 1981 to increase the resources of the branch by increasing by 10 per cent the amount of tax payable over and above 15,000 francs by persons liable for at least 25,000 francs per year in personal income tax. In Belgium, France and Switzerland, greater solidarity in the face of the risk of unemployment was the aim of a contribution levied on civil servants, even though they are not liable to the risk of unemployment. This measure raised serious objections, since it achieves only partial solidarity, in contrast to taxation provided it is reasonably equitable.

The removal of any ceiling on wages for the calculation of enterprise contributions is also a way of improving equity in the sharing of social security costs among the enterprises covered, since it harmonises their liabilities regardless of the distribution of their employees in the wage scale. Attempts have also been made to promote equity between enterprises by the imposition of an equal charge on both, regardless of the proportions of labour and capital they use. But this aim is usually bound up with the desire to lighten the charges on labour-intensive enterprises and promote employment, even at the expense of the resources of social security, at least in the short term. On the other hand, recourse to value added tax is considered by its champions [23] to be the only way of harmonising the financial obligations of enterprises in an objectively equitable manner, while at the same time increasing the income available by broadening the basis of contributions to include that source. Even if only a limited increase in income can be obtained by this measure, especially in the case of enterprises where wages represent the major part of value added, it is nevertheless an attractive one, since it is theoretically the only one combining the advantages of equity and increased yield.

In pluralist schemes, a particular problem of equity arises regarding the financial participation of the various occupational or social categories which are covered by different schemes. Self-employed persons usually have to pay a contribution approximately double that of the employer or employee contribution,[24] possibly subject to a ceiling, allowance being made for flat-rate assessment methods and reductions granted to workers in low income brackets. The flat-rate assessment of income liable to contributions also applies to economically non-active persons. In principle, equity may be said to exist if the same given levels of income liable to contributions give rise to the same obligations and the same benefits. But the problem becomes more complicated when the resources of some schemes are inadequate because of demographic or economic reasons related to the age structure or average occupational income of the group of persons protected. This is true of agricultural schemes which are often financed by revenue from taxes on agricultural produce and assistance from public funds. In this case, a tax on farm produce is supposed to be based partly on the work of the farmers themselves, although there is ambiguity here similar to that involved in equating the enterprise contribution to a deferred wage. More generally, financial compensation machinery[25] has been established between the various schemes to equalise their contribution rates. This is the case in France where the Act of 24 December 1974 was designed to even out disparities among these schemes in the demographic relationship between economically active and non-active persons or the contributing capacity of the protected persons.[26] Such machinery is not detrimental to equity when it covers all protected persons and relates to schemes whose obligations and benefits are harmonised and is thus tantamount to the financial conditions of a unified system. Otherwise, the compensation to be given to schemes with a deficit will be more equitably obtained from public funds.

Some international social security instruments have dealt with the question of financial equity. For example, the ILO's Income Security Recommendation, 1944 (No. 67), provides that "the cost of benefits, including the cost of administration, should be distributed among insured persons, employers and taxpayers, in such a way as to be equitable to insured persons and to avoid hardship to insured persons of small means . . .".[27] Similarly, the ILO's Social Security (Minimum Standards) Convention, 1952 (No. 102), and the European Code of Social Security (1964) of the Council of Europe contain specific provisions in this connection, based on international labour Recommendation No. 67. In accordance with these provisions, which are identical, the methods of financing social security should be such that persons of small means should not have to endure hardship and the economic situation of the classes of persons protected are taken into account. Moreover, the total insurance contributions borne by the employed persons should not exceed 50 per cent of the total financial resources allocated to the protection of employed persons and their wives and children. For the purpose of ascertaining whether this condition is fulfilled, all the benefits provided pursuant to these instruments (except family benefits and, if provided by a special branch, employment injury and occupational disease benefits), may be taken together. Thus, as far as existing international standards are concerned, the equal sharing of financing costs between employed persons on the one hand and employers and the public authorities on the other continues to determine the point at which equity for workers in social security financing begins, in accordance with the original principle of an equal contribution by workers and employers.

FINANCING METHODS AND ECONOMIC POLICY

Any inquiry into the financial rationalisation of social security systems must necessarily take a look at their economic impact with a view to determining the financing methods least prejudicial to the optimum operation of the economy.[28] It is clear that the choice of methods could hardly vary with economic fluctuations without entailing disadvantages. This is no doubt why Beveridge's suggestions concerning the cyclical financing of social security which, like the cyclical government budget, would impose charges varying with the economic situation, have hardly been applied in practice [29] outside unemployment insurance, where the needs do in fact vary according to the current economic situation.[30] However, the financial difficulties of social security due to the crisis have drawn attention to the economic effects of financing methods, especially in relation to employment and international competition. The present circumstances certainly warrant taking into account these two essential aspects, even if it seems preferable to exercise care in tampering with the financial machinery of an institution which, in some countries, draws on resources equivalent at least to those of the government budget.

Employment

As far as employment is concerned, the main objection most often made to the traditional methods of financing has to do with the adverse effects of social costs which, in the form of enterprise contributions, increase the cost of labour and, in a period of recession, discourage enterprises from hiring new workers.[31]

One of the measures commonly used at present for combating unemployment is precisely to reduce or abolish temporarily the contributions payable by employers for certain categories of workers, especially newly hired young workers. In Belgium, this was the purpose of the Act of 24 January 1977 to effect a temporary decrease in social security contributions in order to promote employment, and the Act of 4 August 1978 respecting economic reorientation, which extended the provisions of the previous Act. In France, the national schemes providing for training-cum-employment contracts for young people contain similar measures, which also exist in Italy. The renewal and extension of these measures, especially in France, within the framework either of solidarity contracts (which link early retirement for older workers or reduced hours of work with the recruitment of new employees) or of training contracts (to promote apprenticeship), or in order to assist certain economic sectors or cushion the effect of increases in the minimum wage on the social charges of enterprises, seem to indicate that a lasting reform of social security financing whereby the same objectives could be achieved would be more appropriate than temporary abatements which reduce the normal income of the schemes and make it necessary to draw on public funds.

Reductions in contributions have also been allowed to protected persons and enterprises in order to encourage regional development. For example in Greece, starting in 1955, the rates of contributions for sickness and pensions insurance were reduced by 10 and 20 per cent respectively for insured persons and employers in industrial and handicraft enterprises in certain distressed areas, in order to lower the cost of labour and improve the employment situation, one-third of the reduction being for the workers and two-thirds for the employers. In 1973 the reductions were increased from 10 to 20 per cent and 20 to 40 per cent respectively. Similarly, in Norway enterprise contributions are differentiated by region and in the light of industrial policy, varying in inverse proportion to public regional development subsidies. In Panama, contribution rates are higher in banana-growing areas than in other, less developed, areas. In Yugoslavia, they vary from one republic or autonomous region to another.

In the opposite case, where supply exceeds demand for employment, these methods are the more appropriate since they favour mechanisation and productivity. Even if it is doubtful whether a sound solution of the problem of employment in the industrialised countries might lead to a slowdown in the progress of productivity, it nevertheless seems advisable in the present circumstances to reduce existing inequalities due to the incidence of enterprise contributions which have no particular economic justification. In this respect, a simple and effective solution would be to lift or even do away with the ceiling set for enterprise contributions. By abolishing any ceiling for the assessment of enterprise contributions, it would be possible to eliminate the anomaly of taxing differently, for purposes of social security contributions, the same factor of production on the basis of labour wages alone, encouraging the use of overtime to the detriment of part-time work. This would thus help to promote a more equitable distribution of labour, which would seem likely to improve the employment situation.

It should also be asked whether this harmonisation of employers' social security obligations should be carried further in order to align more closely enterprise costs as well, regardless of the labour or capital intensity of their production processes. Measures along these lines have already been adopted in Belgium for the benefit of small and medium-sized enterprises and projects have been put forward in Belgium, France and Norway to help labour-intensive industries by reducing their social security contributions. Some economists, however, have reservations about such approaches since they consider either that it is not a problem of internal competition between the various economic sectors or that capital-intensive industries are often those which, because of their technological lead and high productivity, are able to gain an advantageous position in the international marked.[32]

These approaches are also open to criticism because of their complexity and the difficulties necessarily involved in applying them, as well as the absence of any clear indication of their meeting the need for greater equity among the enterprises themselves. Sound rationalisation should, on the contrary, help considerably to simplify the financial administration and management of social security. A proposal along these lines recently made in France suggested that enterprises should be totally exempt from contributions to sickness insurance for workers below a certain threshold of remuneration. The measure, which would be simple to apply and general in scope, was intended to benefit above all small and medium-sized labour-intensive firms where low earners predominate, and thus to encourage them to increase the number of their employees.

At the same time, however, the approach usually taken is not satisfactory since the unequal treatment of enterprises in connection with social security costs seems to be a fortuitous consequence of their production processes and not the result of a rational economic choice. Moreover, on the whole it is harmful to employment since the advanced technology sectors favoured by contribution-based financing are often those using little manpower. In these circumstances, standardisation of employers' financing obligations would give back to social security some economic neutrality in relation to the various factors of production, leaving it to economic policy to intervene deliberately in this field through its regulatory machinery, including, where necessary, a deliberate differentiation in contribution rates according to economic activities.

Lastly, from the standpoint of neutrality–and also of equity in the assessment of enterprises' social security payments–it has been thought that the tax approach which was devised for economic reasons for the benefit of public finance could also serve for social finance. On the basis of this precedent, it has been recommended that in social security financing, enterprise contributions should be replaced partially by the value added tax. Although theoretically attractive, this approach raises difficult problems regarding the transfer of costs, which have been studied in Belgium,[33] France,[34] the Federal Republic of Germany[35] and the Netherlands,[36] at the request of the governments concerned or on the initiative of experts, but have rarely been satisfactorily solved. It should be noted in this connection that under the Belgian Act of 29 June 1981 the fraction corresponding to the contribution reduction established for employers of manual workers, amounting to 6.17 per cent of the payroll, is not replaced directly by the value added tax but by receipts from the general budget. This compensation will be made by means of an increase in the value added tax, so designed as to limit its incidence on the price of major consumer goods and services.

In France, for the execution of the Eighth Plan, the Industrial Commission for the Plan has proposed that the contribution base should gradually be extended to the value added by firms in order to clarify the transfer of costs between the various social security schemes and branches and to prevent the undesirable effects of removing the ceiling on wage-based contributions for industries employing a high percentage of white-collar workers where the wages are high and which are precisely the industries that need to be encouraged.

The studies carried out in France [37] show that such a replacement would probably have a favourable effect on employment in the medium term but that this effect would be truly significant only if it were accompanied by a revision of value added tax deductibility in connection with investment.[38]

It would therefore seem that the decision to replace enterprise contributions partially by the value added tax should be only one element in a broader tax reform directed towards a development of employment. At all events, the importance of what is at stake warrants a continuation of the studies undertaken in various countries, preferably within the framework of a programme co-ordinated at the international level. At its meeting at the Council of Europe in Strasbourg on 6 and 7 March 1979, the Conference of European Ministers Responsible for Social Security agreed that a more thorough study should be made of the various techniques of financing social security systems, especially as regards the relationship between workers' and employers' contributions and the State's share or the possible extension of traditional techniques through graduated income taxation by means of direct or indirect taxes. In a memorandum entitled "A Community response to the problem of unemployment", the Commission of the European Communities has recommended five guidelines for an employment strategy, including the reduction of financial constraints on growth. In this respect, it suggests that consideration should be given to alternative approaches more propitious for promoting employment than social security payroll contributions.

International competition

Another important aspect of the economic effects of social security financing has to do with the competitive capacity of the economy in international trade, which also exerts an influence on the level of employment. When trade is liberalised, that capacity is challenged not only on foreign markets but on the domestic market as well. It is not surprising therefore that the concern to limit or harmonise social costs is at least as old as social security and has been constantly present except during periods when social protection developed behind a strict protectionist policy, such as the first German social insurance schemes at the end of the nineteenth century. This concern has become keener since the return to economic liberalism during the initial stages of the creation of the Common Market by the countries of the European Economic Community (EEC). In the absence of the harmonisation of social security systems or at least of their financing methods, some of these countries have tried to obtain scattered competitive advantages, either through transfers between sources of funds, especially from enterprise contributions to the government budget for family benefits, or through temporary or permanent reductions in employers' contributions. In a period of economic crisis, the problem created by such practices is likely to grow worse, above all when the developing countries, profiting from the relative advantage procured from their low level of social costs, step up their industrial production and activity on the international market. As a result, the idea of harmonising social legislation, either between the member countries of the EEC or with respect to Third World countries, has been gaining ground again. The negotiations for the renewal of the Convention of Lomé between the Associated States of Africa, the Caribbean and the Pacific approached the question of observance of basic social standards in the developing countries with the twofold aim of extending social rights and aligning competitive conditions. This question–the question of "social clauses"–was not settled by the new Convention, but it is significant that the name given it was an allusion to the historical debates on the "workers' clauses" that accompanied the framing of the ILO Constitution.[39]

Given the economic importance of the problem of international competition, not only for the trade balance but also for improving the employment situation, financial rationalisation should seek the financing means best calculated to limit its scope. Since the difficulties are due essentially to the social costs involved in enterprise contributions, any proposal to increase individual contributions or to draw on public funds for a better distribution of resources or a more equitable apportionment of costs would facilitate the solution of the problem. Replacement of enterprise contributions by the value added tax would tend in the same direction, although without altering the economic nature of the receipts because of the tax refund in the case of exportation. Among the member countries of the EEC, such replacement should doubtless be co-ordinated because of the effects it would have on competitive conditions. The current position of the Commission of the European Communities in this regard is the result of two decisions. On 19 December 1979, the Commission decided to open the procedure provided for in Article 93 (2) of the Treaty of Rome in connection with the partial sickness insurance taxation system for Italian industry, where contribution rates are differentiated for male and female workers. It found that the larger contribution reduction for female workers was tantamount to government aid within the meaning of Article 92 (1) since it favours industries with a high intensity of female labour, especially the textile, clothing and footwear sectors. The same procedure was brought into operation in connection with measures taken in France to lighten social charges in the textile and clothing sectors. Secondly, in the decision it adopted on 15 September 1980 regarding the substitution in part of taxation for employers' contributions to the Italian sickness insurance scheme, the Commission stated that it was not opposed to the collection of certain social contributions in Italy by means of taxation provided it was applied uniformly to industry as a whole. It is only under these conditions that the taxation system is of a sufficiently general nature not to be regarded as government aid but as a general economic measure. In the EEC, agreement would be facilitated, from a technical point of view, by the harmonisation of the structure and basis of value added tax now being undertaken. Co-ordination would be desirable as well on a larger scale, for example within the framework of the Council of Europe, which has also started to study problems of social security financing, or of the Organisation for Economic Co-operation and Development, which has begun to analyse the relation-ships between tax systems and social security systems. Such co-ordination, however, would also be rendered more difficult by the lack of harmonis-ation between tax systems and the inadequacy of institutional machinery for international co-operation.[40]

CONCLUSION

The various aspects of financial rationalisation related to a selective appropriation of resources, an equitable apportionment of costs and an optimum relation between financing methods and economic policy objec-tives are not of equal concern to all social security financing systems. Appreciable differences exist in this respect between budgetary systems, general or special, and autonomous systems, unified or diversified. How-ever, none of these systems can afford at present to overlook the prospects of rationalisation open to it, possibilities that need be taken advantage of not only because of the financing difficulties besetting most schemes but also because of an economic situation in which priority must be given to measures for developing employment and because of the orientation of social policies towards the elimination of inequalities, encouraging the search for equity in the assessment of both social security contributions and taxes.

As the systems exist in practice, the trends of financial rationalisation obey two contrary approaches, the one aimed at the integration of the social security budget in the general government budget and the other at the adap-tation of the traditional conception of financial autonomy.

There are two variants to the first approach, one directed at obtaining the necessary social security resources from the general revenue of the State or local communities, according to the Australian, Danish or New Zealand model,[41] and the other at drawing up a special budget of earmarked receipts, according to the Soviet model, which has influenced other countries of Eastern Europe, Bulgaria and Czechoslovakia in particular.

The first variant enjoys the advantages of equity, in so far as this characterises the taxation system and the means it provides for the spread-ing of charges through the various general or local tax channels. On the other hand, it is a very heavy burden on government budgets and makes it more difficult to adapt social security financing to changing needs.[42] This accounts for the fact that this variant, despite the wholly logical notion of financing the social function of the public authorities directly by means of public funds, is not at all widespread, except in certain specific social security sectors, such as the provision of medical care of a guaranteed social compensatory income or a social minimum income. Even in Denmark, it has been called in question by the work of a government commission set up to study ways and means of reforming social security financing, which decided in favour of a rational diversification of methods of collection for social purposes.

The second variant (where there is also public financing but under a specific budget utilising earmarked receipts) is more flexible and more easily adjustable to needs in the light of the economic effects of the various financing methods used, which may draw on general public funds, ear-marked taxes or contributions, or contributions based on the income of the persons protected. Furthermore, this variant is quite compatible with a diversified system of financing, either for the benefit of specific occupational and social categories, such as the additional budget for agricultural social benefits in France, or for specific sectors of social security, as in certain countries of Eastern Europe.

In the second approach, which consists in the maintenance of an autonomous system of financing, there are also two variants according to whether the system is unified or diversified. Here too, the unified system is the more infrequent variant but it is also simpler in respect of rationalisation, since the rationalisation requirements must be met in the global context of the system rather than in each sector considered separately. The second variant–the diversified autonomous system of financing–is more widespread, as it conforms more closely to the traditional conception and is also more open to every form of rationalisation adaptable to the needs and capacities of the sectors and schemes concerned, from the standpoint of the national co-ordination of social security financing methods.

In view of the diversity of the systems, it is essential to realise that the development of social security–its capacity to cope with growing costs and also to meet, more fairly and effectively, the constant demands made on it, particularly in regard to the reduction of social inequalities and the strengthening of national solidarity–will henceforth depend on financial rationalisation. It will furthermore be necessary from now on to obtain an overall picture of the general government budget and the social budget–where the latter is separate from the former–and to ensure compatibility between taxation and social security charges, in the interest of taxpayers and contributors and in a concern to organise the economic impact of both, in the manner most beneficial to the economy, as was sensibly recommended by the Council of Europe in a recent report on the prospects for a European social policy for the next ten years.[43] The need to work out a new social security financial doctrine, based on rational principles and adjusted to the problems facing the system, is a matter requiring the general attention of governments and the competent international organisations.

The contribution of international organisations, within the framework of the periodic statistical inquiry of the ILO on the cost of social security [44] or the work of the Commission of the European Communities for the preparation of the European social budget,[45] has proved very useful for a comparative analysis of social receipts and expenditure by branch or function. However, appreciable as they are, if such fact-finding instruments are to serve effective concerted action at the international level, an in-depth study of financial systems will have to be made to update the data collected by the ILO on various occasions (particularly for the First European Regional Conference of States Members of the ILO and at the request of the Commission of the European Communities).[46] As well as a recent study by the International Social Security Association,[47] research is now under way on the subject in the group for the co-ordination of social protection policies of the Commission of the European Communities and the Council of Europe, following the first Conference of European Ministers Responsible for Social Security. If these studies and research are pursued in depth, preferably in a co-ordinated manner, they should not only facilitate an appraisal of new methods of financing conducive to a quantitative and qualitative improvement of social levies but may also open up a new way towards the harmonisation of conceptions and structures of social security financing. Wide dissemination of their results would help to inform the interested parties and to facilitate acceptance of the necessary sacrifices. The inclusion among parliamentary duties of the examination and adaption of social security budgets and accounts, and the institution of special commissions, such as the Commission on Social Security Accounts in France, will promote informed discussion of the problems involved, thus providing democratic guidance for the rationalisation of social security financing.

Notes

[1] For example, the first Austrian scheme for employment injury coverage, introduced by an Act of 28 December 1887, required contributions from workers whose wages exceeded a specific amount. That contribution was equal to one-tenth of the employer's contribution.

[2] The German Government had originally proposed a non-contributory pension scheme, financed wholly out of public funds according to the conception initially prevailing in several Nordic countries and members of the British Commonwealth at the end of the nineteenth century. That conception was in line with the demands made by workers' organisations.

[3] Francis Netter: "Dépréciation monétaire et sécurité sociale" (Colloque sur l'histoire de la sécurité sociale, Bordeaux, 17 and 18 April 1979), in *Actes du 104e Congrès national des sociétés savantes* (Paris, Association pour l'étude de l'histoire de la sécurité sociale, 1980), p. 103.

[4] The initial legislative model for social security, the New Zealand Act of 14 September 1938, under which the financing of the new system was unified largely on the basis of an additional contribution to income tax, hardly had any influence abroad in this connection. However, the use of fiscal services for levying contributions was adopted for certain branches, especially in the Netherlands and the United States in respect of pension insurance, and in Norway and the United Kingdom generally.

[5] The first national pensions schemes developed on the basis of previous non-contributory pensions schemes, which were established in Sweden in 1913 and in Norway in 1926, were financed out of public funds and by means of a contribution proportional to the assessable income of individuals and corporate bodies.

[6] For example the Belgian Act of 23 December 1974 introduced a supplementary car insurance premium to finance the medical care scheme. In Brazil, the planning authorities announced an increase in consumption taxes to reduce the social security deficit.

[7] For example, the economic recovery measures adopted by the Italian Government on 4 February 1977 included a modification of the basis for assessing employers' social security contributions in the form of a partial transfer of contributions, amounting to 100,000 million lire, to the value added tax. In Belgium, similarly, under an Act of 21 December 1977, amended by the Act of 5 August 1978, a charge was imposed on revenue from excise duties and the value added tax on manufactured tobacco for the benefit of the medical care scheme. Subsequently, the Act of 29 June 1981 provided for a reduction of 6.17 per cent of wages in the contributions of enterprises employing manual workers, the State having to make good the corresponding deficit from general receipts by increasing the value added tax. A Royal Decree of 30 June 1981 extended the same reduction to the special schemes for miners and the merchant navy. Lastly, in Argentina, under Acts Nos. 22-293 and 22-294 of 30 September 1980, employers' contributions to the pensions scheme and the National Housing Fund were replaced by a fraction of the value added tax, beginning on 1 October 1980.

[8] Martin B. Tracy: "Contributions under social security programmes: survey in some selected countries", in *International Social Security Review* (Geneva), No. 1, 1976, pp. 66-85.

[9] In its report of 17 October 1979 reviewing the development of social security since 23 May 1972, the National Labour Council in Belgium stated that a redefinition of the financial liabilities of the State, employers, workers and applicants for benefits was a prerequisite for working out a new financial doctrine of social security.

[10] This was not the case in all the schemes at the outset. In the first German sickness insurance scheme, for example, two-thirds of the contributions were paid by the workers and one-third by the employers.

[11] This formula has generally been maintained in Austria, Canada, the Federal Republic of Germany, Japan, Switzerland and the United States in particular.

[12] Exceptionally, the contributions of the protected persons are higher than those of employers in the pension insurance scheme in the Netherlands and account for the bulk of the funds in Yugoslavia.

[13] This is the situation in the Bahamas, Bolivia, Colombia, Cyprus, the Dominican Republic, El Salvador, the German Democratic Republic, Guatemala, Guyana, Honduras, Hungary, India, the Islamic Republic of Iran, Iraq, Jamaica, the Libyan Arab Jamahiriya, Malta, Mauritius, Pakistan, Paraguay, the United Kingdom and Venezuela, where employment injury coverage is financed jointly with sickness insurance schemes, pension insurance schemes or all social insurance schemes.

[14] Brittain: "The incidence of social security payroll taxes", op. cit.

[15] Leuthold: "The incidence of payroll tax in the United States", op. cit.

[16] Council of Europe: *Financing of social security*, op. cit.

[17] Such a sharing of financial liability between the protected persons and the State obtains in the financing of medical care schemes in Australia and Switzerland. The individual contributions to these schemes, however, continue to be flat-rate contributions. Under numerous projects for reforming sickness insurance worked out in Switzerland over the past ten years, however, the existing mutualist conception generally tends to be replaced by individual income-linked contributions. But pending the adoption of one of these projects, the effects of any reduction in government subsidies run counter to the search for equity.

[18] The Income Security Recommendation, 1944 (No. 67), adopted by the International Labour Conference in Philadelphia on 12 May 1944, still linked the allocation of family allow-

ances to social assistance schemes: "Society should normally co-operate with parents through general measures of assistance designed to secure the well-being of dependent children" (Paragraph 28).

[19] The first Swiss unemployment insurance scheme established by the Federal Decree of 29 October 1919 was financed equally by employers, the cantons and the Confederation.

[20] The first unemployment protection schemes set up in Great Britain in 1911 within the trade union framework, before social insurance techniques had been applied to this branch, were often financed solely by the workers on the ground that unemployment was an inevitable economic hazard and it was up to the victims themselves to take the necessary precautions against it. Subsequently, recognition of the principle of "subsidised freedom" led the State and local communities to subsidise relief funds of trade union origin, after the example of the Municipal Councils of Liège in 1897 and of Ghent in 1899.

[21] Alain and Chantal Euzéby: "A propos du plafond des cotisations de sécurité sociale", op. cit.

[22] Mention should be made in this respect of the original approach taken by the Norwegian scheme, where a total contribution of 5.3 per cent for employed persons and of 10.2 per cent for self-employed workers on occupational earnings subject to a ceiling is combined with a contribution of 4.4 per cent on total assessable income, primarily to finance medical care.

[23] The first suggestion of this kind appears to have come from the United States: "Suggestions have been made from time to time as to other bases on which the employers' contribution might be assessed, and I think these are worthy of more attention than they have hitherto received. . . . Professor Colm has recently suggested that the tax should be assessed on the value added by the firm rather than by reference to the number of workers employed." E. M. Burns: "Can social insurance provide social security?", in *Social security in the United States*, record of the Eighth National Conference on Social Security, New York City, 26 and 27 April 1935 (New York, American Association for Social Security, 1935).

[24] This is not necessarily the case when the self-employed workers are covered by special schemes.

[25] J. C. F. C. Chadelat: "La compensation", in *Droit social*, Special issue, Nos. 9-10, 1976, pp. 85-115.

[26] These two aspects are taken into account for compensation between schemes for wage earners, whereas only the demographic relationship is considered for compensation between these schemes and schemes for self-employed workers. It should be mentioned here that the Industrial Commission of the Planning Commissariat proposed for the execution of the Eighth Plan (1981-85), before the recent decision to modify its duration and implementation, that the contribution of the general industrial and commercial workers' scheme to the other schemes should be limited to demographic compensation in order to prevent a dangerous spiral in social security costs, which are borne largely by the industrial sector.

[27] Annex, paragraph 26. The suggestions made for the application of these guiding principles specify that employers, besides covering compensation for employment injuries, should contribute half the total cost of benefits confined to employed persons, while the community should bear the cost of benefits which cannot be met by contributions, such as benefits granted to persons entering into insurance when already elderly, maternity benefits, basic invalidity, old-age and survivors' benefits, long-term unemployment benefits and protection for self-employed persons of small means.

[28] ILO: *L'impact macro-économique de la sécurité sociale* (Geneva, 1970); and Commission of the European Communities: *The economic impact of social security*, Social Policy Series, No. 21 (Brussels, 1970).

[29] However, section 3 of the British National Insurance Act of 1 August 1946 retained Beveridge's suggestion in the following terms: "Where it appears to the Treasury expedient so to do with a view to maintaining a stable level of employment, they may by order direct that contributions, instead of being paid at the rates set out in the First Schedule to the Act, shall, for such periods as may be specified by or determined in accordance with the order, be paid at such higher or lower rates . . . as may be so specified or determined."

[30] The Secretary-General of the General Confederation of Labour–*Force Ouvrière* recently proposed that the unemployment insurance deficit should be met by means of a 15-year loan, in the hope that its redemption would take place in more auspicious economic circumstances. On 9 September 1981, the French Government decided to launch a loan of 6,000 million francs for this purpose.

[31] See Colin D. Campbell (ed.): *Financing social security* (Washington, DC, American Enterprise Institute for Public Policy Research, 1979), p. 34.

[32] Euzéby: "Financement de la sécurité sociale et emploi", op. cit. See also Ch. 3 above.

[33] J. Mateljan: "Modes alternatifs de financement de la sécurité sociale", in *Revue belge de sécurité sociale* (Brussels), Oct. 1976; Frank: "Substitution de la valeur ajoutée aux salaires...", op. cit.; Deleeck: "Un autre mode de financement de la sécurité sociale: des cotisations calculées sur la valeur ajoutée", op. cit.; and Conseil national du travail: *Rapport concernant une modification éventuelle du calcul des cotisations de la sécurité sociale* (Brussels, 30 Apr. 1980).

[34] Ch. Rollet: "Pourquoi modifier l'assiette des cotisations sociales?", in *Problèmes économiques* (Paris), 21 Feb. 1979, pp. 14-20; and M. C. Caravel: "Le pour et le contre d'un élargissement de l'assiette des cotisations patronales à la valeur ajoutée", in *Questions de sécurité sociale* (Paris), No. 3, 1980, pp. 41-46.

[35] Inquiry of the Committee on Transfers, 1981.

[36] De Neubourg and Caspers: *Social security system financing: Charges on the net value added and other alternatives in the Netherlands*, op. cit.

[37] The consequences of such a reform on employment were analysed in a report of the General Planning Commissariat dated 6 July 1977. According to the report, the partial transfer of social security costs to taxes, whether the income tax or the value added tax, would lead to some improvement in the employment situation after a period of five years. A similar conclusion was reached by the Economic and Social Council of France in the opinion it gave on 6 December 1978 concerning Mr. Corentin Calvez's report; see *Journal officiel de la République française* (Avis et rapports du Conseil économique et social), 9 Feb. 1979, pp. 225-256.

[38] Patrick Artus, Henri Sterdyniak and Pierre Villa: "L'incidence de la suppression de la cotisation sociale des employeurs: un essai de mesure", in *Problèmes économiques*, 27 May 1981, pp. 7-14.

[39] The measures called for by a recent congress of the Swedish Federation of Clothing, Textile and Footwear Workers, which met in Stockholm from 23 to 28 August 1981, are indicative of the concerns of trade unions in developed countries, especially in the sectors most affected by international trade. The Federation called, in particular, for the inclusion in commercial contracts of a special clause allowing, subject to agreed conditions, for the limitation of imports from countries where trade union rights are not respected, where there is no minimum wage or where children are required to work at an age below that permitted by international standards. In the same vein, the trade unions and occupational organisations in the textile and clothing sectors of the EEC stated on 26 October 1981 that the next agreement concerning international trade in textiles should favour the poorest producer countries that apply ILO social standards.

[40] Alain Euzéby: "Développement de la sécurité sociale et nouvel ordre économique international", in *Cahiers de la Faculté des sciences économiques de Grenoble* (Grenoble), No. 1, 1981, pp. 101-121.

[41] Obviously only highly representative but not entirely representative models exist of the variants chosen for illustrating unified systems, since completely unified financing systems are rare.

[42] A. Euzéby: "Faut-il fiscaliser la sécurité sociale?", op. cit.

[43] Laroque, Leaper and Pfaff: *Prospects for an economic and social policy for the next ten years*, op. cit.

[44] ILO: *The cost of social security*, op. cit.

[45] Commission of the European Communities: *The European Social Budget, 1980-1975-1970* (Luxembourg, Office for Official Publications of the European Communities, 1978).

[46] ILO: *The financing of social security*, op. cit.; and European Economic Community: *Financement de la sécurité sociale dans les pays de la CEE*, study prepared by the ILO at the request of the Commission of the EEC in collaboration with the Directorate General of Social Affairs, Social Policy Series, No. 5 (Brussels, 1962).

[47] ISSA: *Methods of social security financing*, op. cit.